Read This, It's Funny!!

Ralph,
I hope you enjoy this.
We could all use a laugh.

Carl

Read This; It's Funny!!

Compiled By
Carl E. Knox

OCGI
Portland, OR
www.laughableemail.com

Read This; It's Funny!!
A Laughable E-mail Collection
Compiled by Carl E. Knox

Published by:
Our Computer Guy, Inc.
2000 N.E. 42nd Ave, Ste 101
Portland, OR 97213 U.S.A.
http://www.laughableemail.com

Library of Congress Cataloging-in-Publication Data

Library of Congress Control Number: 2003101131

ISBN 0-972844-50-3

Printed and bound in the United States of America.

To all of the givers and receivers.

Read This, It's Funny!!

Preface vii
That's Punny 1
Subject: Mr. & Mrs. Potato 2
Subject: Puns 3
Subject: Working Puns 4
Subject: Even More Puns 5
Subject: Still More Puns 7
Subject: There Was This Guy 8
Subject: The Hills 9
Subject: What Does She Do? 11
Children 12
Subject: Please Egcuse My Child 13
Subject: Kids on Relationships 15
Subject: Kid Wisdom 18
Subject: Science Exam Quotes 19
Subject: Really Awfully Bad Writing 22
Is It That Time Already? 23
Subject: The Night Before Thanksgiving 24
Subject: Merry Christmas, Legally Speaking 26
Subject: A Christmas Poem 27
Subject: The Month After Christmas 29
Subject: 12 Days of Christmas 30
Subject: I Think Santa Claus is a Woman.... 35
Subject: Santa and the Angel 37
Subject: Santa's New Contract 38
Subject: Thanksgiving Weather 40
Subject: What Moms REALLY Want 41
Family 42
Subject: Before Children/After Children 43
Subject: Cost of Kids 45
Subject: Just a Mother 47
Subject: Lesson for the Day 49
Subject: Mustard 50
Subject: Potty Humor 51
Subject: Somebody Said 52
Subject: Things Your Mother Wouldn't Say 54
Subject: Why Parents Have Gray Hair 55
Subject: Christmas Intent 56

Read This; It's Funny!!

Take Action **57**
Subject: Deteriorata 58
Subject: Instructions for Life 60
Subject: Try This 62
Signs of the Times **63**
Subject: Bumper Stickers 1 64
Subject: Bumper Stickers 2 67
Subject: Cute Signs 68
Subject: Women's T-Shirts 70
Subject: Actual Headlines 71
Subject: T-Shirt Slogans 72
Subject: Rejected Hallmark Cards 75
Answer This **76**
Subject: Brain Exercise 77
Subject: Jedi Mind Trick 79
Subject: Quick Eye Exam 81
Glorified Calculators **82**
Subject: Computer Gender 83
Subject: Computer Haiku 84
Subject: Dr. Seuss Tech 86
Subject: LAZY Virus 87
Subject: Remember When 88
Subject: Spell Checker 89
Subject: Who's on Start? 90
Subject: Windows Southern Edition 92
Our Jokes, Ourselves **94**
Subject: Blond Revenge 95
Subject: Jail 96
Subject: Hero 97
Subject: Rod and Reel 98
Subject: Special Pig 99
Subject: Pillsbury Doughboy 100
Subject: Right Age for Cussing 101
Subject: How to Handle Stress 102
How Things Get Done **103**
Subject: How to Annoy People 104
Subject: How to Screw Up an Interview 106
Subject: How To Keep A Healthy Level Of Insanity 108
Subject: 10 Ways To Terrify A Telemarketer 109
Information You Can Use **110**
Subject: Anagrams 111
Subject: Broker's Tips 112

Contents

Subject: Cat Wisdom 113
Subject: Chocolate is a Vegetable 114
Subject: Daffynitions 115
Subject: More Daffynitions 116
Subject: New Dog Cross Breeds 118
Subject: Gender 120
Subject: Questions for the Wise 122
Subject: Rules for Writers 123
Subject: Today's Stock Market Report 125
Subject: Weather by Degree 126
Subject: The Y1K Crisis 128
Are You One? **129**
Subject: Do You Have A.A.A.D.D? 130
Subject: You Know You're Not a Kid Anymore If 131
Subject: You Worked During the 90's If 132
Subject: You've Been Out of College Too Long When 134
Dear Sir or Madam **135**
Subject: Letter to a Bank 136
Subject: Letter to the IRS 139
Subject: Stewart to Bombeck 142
On Being Married **144**
Subject: Behind Every Great Inventor 145
Subject: Buy It! 146
Subject: Fore!!! 148
Subject: Heart to Heart 149
Subject: What's in the Box 150
Subject: To Be Six, Again 151
Subject: Marriage Quotes 152
Men and Women **153**
Subject: Because I'm A Guy 154
Subject: Differences Between a Man and a Woman 156
Subject: Discoveries of the Sexes 157
Subject: How-to Classes For Men 158
Subject: Moods of a Woman 160
Subject: Open Letter to Women 161
Subject: Raging River 163
Subject: On the Next Edition of "Survivor" 164
Subject: Top Ten 165
Subject: Why It's Great to be a Man... 166
Subject: Perfection 168
Subject: Young King Arthur 169
Subject: Tech Support 171

Read This; It's Funny!!

Quips **172**
Subject: Airlines 173
Subject: Mutterings 175
Subject: Exercise is Good For You... 176
Subject: Birthdays and Time 177
Subject: Life Quips 178
Subject: Little Hints and Sayings 179
Subject: More Wisdom 181
Subject: Politically Correct Ways to Call Someone Stupid . 182
Subject: Some Things For You to Ponder... 183
Subject: Ponder This 2 184
Subject: Sarcastic Remarks to Get You Through the Day .. 186
Subject: Still More Quips 188
Subject: Useful Conflict Resolution Phrases 189
Subject: Wisdom of Will Rogers 190
Subject: Words of Wisdom 191
Old Humor **192**
Subject: Found Money 193
Subject: Benefits of Being a Senior 194
Subject: Getting Old 196
Subject: Car Jacker 197
Subject: Senior Driver 198
Subject: Those People from Maine 199
Subject: Leonard and the Devil 200
Subject: I'm a Senior Citizen 201
Subject: Wisdom From Senior Citizens 203
Subject: Sharing Everything 205
Jocks Slaps **206**
Subject: Baseball In Heaven? 207
Subject: Golf 208
Subject: Priorities 209
Subject: Sports Geniuses 210
Stories **213**
Subject: My Class Reunion 214
Subject: Michael the Dragon Master 217
Subject: Email From Heaven 218
Subject: Bad Day 219
Subject: Moving to Arizona 220
Subject: Please Help 222
Subject: Snow 224
Subject: Rat Race Explained.... 227
Subject: Where's Ethyl? 228

Contents

Subject: Cigars 230

The South **231**

Subject: Movin to Texas? 232

Subject: Redneck Etiquette 235

Subject: Redneck Valentines Day Poem 237

Subject: Southern Advice.................................... 240

Subject: Southern Expressions 242

Subject: Girls Raised in the South 243

Subject: Southern Knowledge 246

Subject: Texas First Aid..................................... 248

Subject: You Know You're a Texan When 249

Subject: You Might be a Redneck Jedi if..... 251

Subject: It's a Texas Thing.. 252

Words of Wisdom **253**

Subject: Brilliant 254

Subject: Great Truths For Adults........................ 257

Subject: Zen 258

History **260**

Subject: Class of 2002 261

Subject: Good Old Days 263

All of Your Business **265**

Subject: New Element 266

Subject: Annual Christmas Party 267

Subject: Business Sense...................................... 270

Subject: Differences Between You and Your Boss 271

Subject: Heavenly Welcome................................ 272

Subject: Reasons For Not Coming to Work 273

Subject: Restroom Rules 275

Subject: Multi-Cultural Bloopers 276

What We Have Learned **278**

Subject: Rules of Life 279

Subject: Leadership 280

Subject: Take a Letter 281

Index.. **283**

Preface

To: The Reader

From: The Editor

Subject: Read This; It's Funny!!

What you are about to read is a collection of humorous e-mails that have been read and forwarded, by people like you, to friends, and family, all over the world.

They are the type of jokes, stories, and one-liners that beg to be shared.

It is hoped that you will enjoy reading them.

Included is a floppy disk containing every e-mail found in this book. They are stored as text files and, as such, can be opened in any word processor or text editor.

Please feel free to forward them.

That's Punny

Subject: Mr. & Mrs. Potato 2
Subject: Puns 3
Subject: Working Puns 4
Subject: Even More Puns 5
Subject: Still More Puns 7
Subject: There Was This Guy 8
Subject: The Hills 9
Subject: What Does She Do? 11

Read This, It's Funny!

Subject: Mr. & Mrs. Potato

You know that all potatoes have eyes. Well, Mr. and Mrs. Potato had eyes for each other and they finally got married and had a little one... a real Sweet Potato, whom they called "Yam." They wanted the best for little Yam, telling her all about the facts of life.

They warned her about going out and getting Half Baked because she could get Mashed, get a bad name like "Hot Potato," and then end up with a bunch of Tater Tots.

She said, "Not to worry, no Mr. McSpud could get me in the sack and make a Rotten Potato out of me!" But she wouldn't stay home and become a Couch Potato either. She would get plenty of food and exercise so as not to be skinny like her Shoestring cousins.

Mr. and Mrs. Potato even told her about going off to Europe and to watch out for the greasy guys from France called the French Fries.

They also said she should watch out for the Indians when going out west because she could get Scalloped. Mr. and Mrs. Potato wanted the best for Yam, so they sent her to Idaho P.U., that's Potato University, where the Big Potatoes come from. When she graduates, she'll really be in the Chips.

But one day she came home and said she was going to marry Tom Brokaw. Mr. and Mrs. Potato were very upset and said she couldn't marry him because he's just a.......

Are you ready for this?

Are you sure?

This is REEeeeeeally bad!

OK! Here it is! Remember I warned you!!!

COMMON TATER!!!!!!!!!

Subject: Puns

Evidence has been found that William Tell and his family were avid bowlers. However, all the league records were unfortunately destroyed in a fire. Thus we'll never know for whom the Tells bowled.

A man rushed into the doctor's office and shouted, "Doctor! I think I'm shrinking!!" The doctor calmly responded, "Now, settle down. You'll just have to be a little patient."

A marine biologist developed a race of genetically engineered dolphins that could live forever if they were fed a steady diet of seagulls. One day his supply of the birds ran out, so he had to go out and trap some more. On the way back, he spied two lions asleep on the road. Afraid to wake them, he gingerly stepped over them. Immediately, he was arrested and charged with transporting gulls across sedate lions for immortal porpoises.

A skeptical anthropologist was cataloging South American folk remedies with the assistance of a tribal brujo who indicated that the leaves of a particular fern were a sure cure for any case of constipation. When the anthropologist expressed his doubts, the brujo looked him in the eye and said, "Let me tell you, with fronds like these, who needs enemas?"

Back in the 1800's the Tates Watch Company of Massachusetts wanted to produce other products and, since they already made the cases for pocket watches, decided to market compasses for the pioneers traveling west. It turned out that although their watches were of finest quality, their compasses were so bad that people often ended up in Canada or Mexico rather than California. This, of course, is the origin of the expression, "He who has a Tates is lost!"

A famous Viking explorer returned home from a voyage and found his name missing from the town register. His wife insisted on complaining to the local civic official who apologized profusely saying, "I must have taken Leif off my census."

Read This, It's Funny!

Subject: Working Puns

My first job was working in an orange juice factory, but I got canned... couldn't concentrate.

Then I worked in the woods as a lumberjack, but I just couldn't hack it, so they gave me the ax.

After that I tried to be a tailor, but I just wasn't suited for it... mainly because it was a so-so job.

Next I tried working in a muffler factory, but that was too exhausting.

Then I tried to be a chef — figured it would add a little spice to my life, but I just didn't have the thyme.

I attempted to be a deli worker, but any way I sliced it, I couldn't cut the mustard.

My best job was being a musician, but eventually I found I wasn't noteworthy.

I studied a long time to become a doctor, but I didn't have any patience.

Next was a job in a shoe factory; I tried but I just didn't fit in.

I became a professional fisherman, but discovered that I couldn't live on my net income.

I managed to get a good job working for a pool maintenance company, but the work was just too draining.

So then I got a job in a workout center, but they said I wasn't fit for the job.

After many years of trying to find steady work I finally got a job as a historian, until I realized there was no future in it.

My last job was working at Starbucks, but I had to quit because it was always the same old grind.

SO I RETIRED AND I FOUND I AM PERFECT FOR THE JOB!

Subject: Even More Puns

A mushroom walks into a bar, sits down and orders a drink. The bartender says "We don't serve mushrooms here."

The mushroom says, "Why not? I'm a fun guy!"

A three-legged dog walks into a saloon in the Old West. He sidles up to the bar and announces: "I'm looking for the man who shot my paw."

This guy goes into a restaurant for a Christmas breakfast while in his hometown for the holidays. After looking over the menu he says, "I'll just have the eggs benedict."

His order comes a while later and it's served on a big, shiny hubcap.

He asks the waiter, "What's with the hubcap?"

The waiter sings, "There's no plate like chrome for the hollandaise!"

When she told me I was average, she was just being mean.

A neutron goes into a bar and asks the bartender, "How much for a beer?"

The bartender replies, "For you, no charge."

Two atoms are walking down the street and they run into each other. One says to the other, "Are you all right?"

"No, I lost an electron!"

"Are you sure?"

"Yeah, I'm positive!"

Did you hear about the Buddhist who refused his dentist's novocaine during root canal work? He wanted to transcend dental medication.

A group of chess enthusiasts checked into a hotel and were standing in the lobby discussing their recent tournament victories. After about an hour, the manager came out of the office and asked them to disperse.

"But why?," they asked, as they moved off.

"Because," he said, "I can't stand chess nuts boasting in an open foyer."

A doctor made it his regular habit to stop off at a bar for a hazelnut daiquiri on his way home. The bartender knew of his habit, and would always have the drink waiting at precisely 5:03 p.m. One afternoon, as the end of the workday approached, the bartender was dismayed to find that he was out of hazelnut extract. Thinking quickly, he threw together a daiquiri made with hickory nuts and set it on the bar.

The doctor came in at his regular time, took one sip of the drink and exclaimed, "This isn't a hazelnut daiquiri!"

"No, I'm sorry," replied the bartender, "It's a hickory daiquiri, doc."

A hungry lion was roaming through the jungle looking for something to eat. He came across two men. One was sitting under a tree and reading a book; the other was typing away on his typewriter. The lion quickly pounced on the man reading the book and devoured him. Even the king of the jungle knows that readers digest and writers cramp.

There was a man who entered a local paper's pun contest. He sent in ten different puns, in the hope that at least one of the puns would win. Unfortunately, no pun in ten did.

A guy goes to a psychiatrist. "Doc, I keep having these alternating recurring dreams. First I'm a teepee; then I'm a wigwam; then I'm a teepee; then I'm a wigwam. It's driving me crazy. What's wrong with me?"

The doctor replies: "It's very simple. You're two tents."

A woman has twins, and gives them up for adoption. One of them goes to a family in Egypt and is named "Amal". The other goes to a family in Spain; they name him "Juan". Years later, Juan sends a picture of himself to his mom. Upon receiving the picture, she tells her husband that she wishes she also had a picture of Amal. Her husband responds, "But they are twins—if you've seen Juan, you've seen Amal."

A thief broke into the local police station and stole all the lavatory equipment. A spokesperson was quoted as saying, "We have absolutely nothing to go on."

Subject: Still More Puns

1. Two vultures board an airplane, each carrying two dead raccoons.
The stewardess looks at them and says, "I'm sorry, gentlemen, only one carrion allowed per passenger."
2. Two boll weevils grew up in South Carolina. One went to Hollywood and became a famous actor. The other stayed behind in the cotton fields and never amounted to much. The second one, naturally, became known as the lesser of two weevils.
3. Two Eskimos sitting in a kayak were chilly, but when they lit a fire in the craft, it sank, proving once again that you can't have your kayak and heat it, too.
4. These friars were behind on their belfry payments, so they opened up a small florist shop to raise funds. Since everyone liked to buy flowers from the men of God, a rival florist across town thought the competition was unfair.
He asked the good fathers to close down, but they would not.
He went back and begged the friars to close.
They ignored him.
So, the rival florist hired Hugh MacTaggart, the roughest and most vicious thug in town to "persuade" them to close.
Hugh beat up the friars and trashed their store, saying he'd be back if they didn't close up shop. Terrified, they did so, thereby proving that Hugh, and only Hugh, can prevent florist friars.
5. Mahatma Gandhi, as you know, walked barefoot most of the time, which produced an impressive set of calluses on his feet. He also ate very little, which made him rather frail and with his odd diet, he suffered from bad breath. This made him ....what? (Oh, man, this is so bad, it's good) A super calloused fragile mystic hexed by halitosis.

Subject: There Was This Guy

There was this guy and he had a girlfriend named Lorraine who was very pretty and he liked her a lot.

One day he went to work and found that a new girl had started working there. Her name was Clearly and she was absolutely gorgeous.

He became quite besotted with Clearly and after a while it became obvious that she was interested in him too. But this guy was a loyal man and he wouldn't do anything with Clearly while he was still going out with Lorraine.

He decided that there was nothing left to do but to break up with Lorraine and get it on with Clearly. He planned several times to tell Lorraine but he couldn't bring himself to do it.

Then one day they went for a walk along the river bank when Lorraine slipped and fell into the river.

The current carried her off and she drowned. The guy stopped for a moment by the river and then ran off smiling and singing............

(Are you sure you want to do this?)

"I can see Clearly now Lorraine has gone."

Subject: The Hills

Bob Hill and his new wife, Betty, were vacationing in Europe, as it happens in Transylvania. They were driving a rental car along a rather deserted highway. It was late, and raining very hard. Bob could barely see 10 feet in front of the car. Suddenly the car skids out of control! Bob attempts to control the car, but to no avail! The car swerves and smashes into a tree.

Moments later, Bob shakes his head to clear the fog. Dazed, he looks over at the passenger seat and sees his new wife unconscious, with her head bleeding! Despite the rain and unfamiliar countryside, Bob knows he has to carry her to the nearest phone.

Bob carefully picks his wife up and begins trudging down the road. After a short while, he sees a light. He heads towards the light, which is coming from an old, large house. He approaches the door and knocks. A minute passes. A small, hunched man opens the door. Bob immediately blurts, "Hello, my name is Bob Hill, and this is my wife, Betty. We've been in a terrible accident, and my wife has been seriously hurt. Can I please use your phone??"

"I'm sorry," replies the hunchback, "but we don't have a phone. My master is a doctor. Come in and I will get him."

Bob brings his wife in. An elegant man comes down the stairs. "I'm afraid my assistant may have misled you. I am not a medical doctor. I am a scientist. However, it is many miles to the nearest clinic, and I have had basic medical training. I will see what I can do. Igor, bring them down to the laboratory."

With that, Igor picks up Betty and carries her downstairs, with Bob following closely. Igor places Betty on a table in the lab. Bob collapses from exhaustion and his own injuries; so Igor places Bob on an adjoining table.

After a brief examination, Igor's master looks worried. "Things are serious, Igor. Prepare a transfusion." Igor and his master work feverishly, but to no avail. Bob and Betty Hill are no more.

The Hills' deaths upsets Igor's master greatly. Wearily, he climbs the steps to his conservatory, which houses his pipe organ. For it is here that he has always found solace. He begins to play, and a stirring, almost haunting melody fills the house.

Meanwhile, Igor is still in the lab tidying up. As the music fills the lab, his eyes catch movement, and he notices the fingers

9

on Betty Hill's hand twitch. Stunned, he watches as Bob's arm begins to rise! He is further amazed as Betty sits straight up! Unable to contain himself, he dashes up the stairs to the conservatory. He bursts in and shouts to his master,

"Master, Master!...... The Hills are alive with the sound of music!"

Subject: What Does She Do?

A couple lived near the ocean and used to walk the beach a lot. One summer they noticed a girl who was at the beach pretty much every day. She wasn't unusual, nor was the travel bag she carried, except for one thing; she would approach people who were sitting on the beach, glance around furtively, then speak to them.

Generally the people would respond negatively and she would wander off, but occasionally someone would nod and there would be a quick exchange of money for something she carried in her bag. The couple assumed she was selling drugs and debated calling the cops, but since they didn't know for sure they just continued to watch her.

After a couple of weeks the wife said, "Honey, have you ever noticed that she only goes up to people with boom boxes and other electronic devices?"

He hadn't and said so. Then she said, "Tomorrow I want you to get a towel and our big radio and go lie out on the beach. Then we can find out what she's really doing."

Well, the plan went off without a hitch and the wife was almost hopping up and down with anticipation when she saw the girl talk to her husband and leave.

The man walked up the beach and met his wife at the road. "Well, is she selling drugs?" she asked, excitement pouring out with her voice.

"No, she's not," he said, enjoying this probably more than he should have.

"Well, what is it then? What does she do?" his wife fairly shrieked.

The man grinned and said, "She's a battery salesman."

"A battery salesman?" cried the wife.

"Yes," he replied, "she sells 'C' cells by the sea shore!"

Children

Subject: Please Egcuse My Child 13
Subject: Kids on Relationships 15
Subject: Kid Wisdom 18
Subject: Science Exam Quotes 19
Subject: Really Awfully Bad Writing 22

Subject: Please Egcuse My Child

These are excuse notes from parents (including original spelling) collected by schools from all over the country.

1. My son is under a doctor's care and should not take P.E. today. Please execute him.

2. Please excuse Lisa for being absent. She was sick and I had her shot.

3. Dear School: Please ekscuse John being absent on Jan. 28, 29, 30, 31, 32, and also 33.

4. Please excuse Gloria from Jim today. She is administrating.

5. Please excuse Roland from P.E. for a few days. Yesterday he fell out of a tree and misplaced his hip.

6. John has been absent because he had two teeth taken out of his face.

7. Carlos was absent yesterday because he was playing football. He was hurt in the growing part.

8. Megan could not come to school today because she has been bothered by very close veins.

9. Chris will not be in school cus he has an acre in his side.

10. Please excuse Ray Friday from school. He has very loose vowels.

11. Please excuse Pedro from being absent yesterday. He had (diahre) (dyrea) (direathe) the sh*ts. [words in ()'s were crossed out.]

12. Please excuse Tommy for being absent yesterday. He had diarrhea and his boots leak.

13. Irving was absent yesterday because he missed his bust.

Read This; It's Funny!

14. Please excuse Jimmy for being. It was his father's fault.

15. I kept Billie home because she had to go Christmas shopping because I don't know what size she wears.

16. Please excuse Jennifer for missing school yesterday. We forgot to get the Sunday paper off the porch, and when we found it Monday, we thought it was Sunday.

17. Sally won't be in school a week from Friday. We have to attend her funeral.

18. My daughter was absent yesterday because she was tired. She spent a weekend with the Marines.

19. Please excuse Jason for being absent yesterday. He had a cold and could not breed well.

20. Please excuse Mary for being absent yesterday. She was in bed with gramps.

21. Gloria was absent yesterday as she was having a gangover.

22. Please excuse Burma, she has been sick and under the doctor.

23. Maryann was absent December 11-16, because she had a fever, sore throat, headache and upset stomach. Her sister was also sick, fever and sore throat, her brother had a low grade fever and ached all over. I wasn't the best either, sore throat and fever. There must be something going around, her father even got hot last night.

24. Please excuse little Jimmy for not being in school yesterday. His father is gone and I could not get him ready because I was in bed with the doctor.

Subject: Kids on Relationships

HOW DO YOU DECIDE WHO TO MARRY?
"You got to find somebody who likes the same stuff. Like if you like sports, she should like it that you like sports, and she should keep the chips and dip coming."
Alan, age 10

"No person really decides before they grow up who they're going to marry. God decides it all way before, and you get to find out later who you're stuck with."
Kirsten, age 10

WHAT IS THE RIGHT AGE TO GET MARRIED?
"Twenty-three is the best age because you know the person FOREVER by then."
Camille, age 10

"No age is good to get married at. You got to be a fool to get married."
Freddie, age 6

HOW CAN A STRANGER TELL IF TWO PEOPLE ARE MARRIED?
"Married people usually look happy to talk to other people."
Eddie, age 6

"You might have to guess, based on whether they seem to be yelling at the same kids."
Derrick, age 8

WHAT DO YOU THINK YOUR MOM AND DAD HAVE IN COMMON?
"Both don't want no more kids."
Lori, age 8

WHAT DO MOST PEOPLE DO ON A DATE?
"Dates are for having fun, and people should use them to get to know each other. Even boys have something to say if you listen long enough."
Lynnette, age 8

Read This; It's Funny!

"On the first date, they just tell each other lies, and that usually gets them interested enough to go for a second date."
Martin, age 10

WHAT WOULD YOU DO ON A FIRST DATE THAT WAS TURNING SOUR?

"I'd run home and play dead. The next day I would call all the newspapers and make sure they wrote about me in all the dead columns."
Craig, age 9

WHEN IS IT OK TO KISS SOMEONE?

"When they're rich."
Pam, age 7

"The law says you have to be eighteen, so I wouldn't want to mess with that."
Curt, age 7

"The rule goes like this: if you kiss someone, then you should marry them and have kids with them. It's the right thing to do.
Howard, age 8

IS IT BETTER TO BE SINGLE OR MARRIED?

"I don't know which is better, but I'll tell you one thing. I'm never going to have sex with my wife. I don't want to be all grossed out."
Theodore, age 8

"It's better for girls to be single but not for boys. Boys need someone to clean up after them."
Anita, age 9

"Single is better, for the simple reason that I wouldn't want to change no diapers. Of course, if I did get married, I'd just phone my mother and have her come over for some coffee and diaper-changing."
Kirsten, age 10

HOW WOULD THE WORLD BE DIFFERENT IF PEOPLE DIDN'T GET MARRIED?
"There sure would be a lot of kids to explain, wouldn't there?"
Kelvin, age 8

"You can be sure of one thing - the boys would come chasing after us just the same as they do now."
Roberta, age 7

HOW WOULD YOU MAKE A MARRIAGE WORK?
"If you want to last with your man, you should wear a lot of sexy clothes, especially underwear that is red and maybe has a few diamonds on it."
Lori, age 8

"Tell your wife that she looks pretty even if she looks like a truck."
Ricky, age 10

Read This; It's Funny!

Subject: Kid Wisdom

1. Never trust a dog to watch your food. Patrick, age 10
2. When your dad is mad and asks you, "Do I look stupid?" don't answer him. - Michael, 14
3. Never tell your mom her diet's not working. Michael, 14
4. Stay away from prunes. - Randy, 9
5. Never pee on an electric fence. - Robert, 13
6. Don't squat with your spurs on. - Noronha, 13
7. Don't pull dad's finger when he tells you to. - Emily, 10
8. When your mom is mad at your dad, don't let her brush your hair. - Taylia, 11
9. Never allow your three-year old brother in the same room as your school assignment. - Traci, 14
10. Don't sneeze in front of mom when you're eating crackers. - Mitchell, 12
11. Puppies still have bad breath even after eating a tic tac. - Andrew, 9
12. Never hold a dust buster and a cat at the same time.
- Kyoyo, 9
13. You can't hide a piece of broccoli in a glass of milk.
- Armir, 9
14. Don't wear polka-dot underwear under white shorts.
- Kellie, 11
15. If you want a kitten, start out by asking for a horse.
- Naomi, 15
16. Felt markers are not good to use as lipstick.
- Lauren, 9
17. Don't pick on your sister when she's holding a baseball bat.
- Joel, 10
18 When you get a bad grade in school, show it to your mom when she's on the phone. - Alyesha, 13
19. Never try to baptize a cat. - Eileen, 8

Subject: Science Exam Quotes

Quotes from 11 year olds' Science Exams

"When you breath, you inspire. When you do not breath, you expire."

"H2O is hot water, and CO2 is cold water"

"To collect fumes of sulphur, hold a deacon over a flame in a test tube"

"When you smell an oderless gas, it is probably carbon monoxide"

"Nitrogen is not found in Ireland because it is not found in a free state"

"Water is composed of two gins, Oxygin and Hydrogin. Oxygin is pure gin. Hydrogin is gin and water."

"Three kinds of blood vessels are arteries, vanes and caterpillars."

"Respiration is composed of two acts, first inspiration, and then expectoration."

"The moon is a planet just like the earth, only it is even deader."

"Artifical insemination is when the farmer does it to the cow instead of the bull."

"Dew is formed on leaves when the sun shines down on them and makes them perspire."

"A super-saturated solution is one that holds more than it can hold."

"The body consists of three parts- the brainium, the borax and the abominable cavity. The brainium contains the brain, the borax contains the heart and lungs, and the abominable cavity contains the bowls, of which there are five - a, e, i, o, and u."

"The pistol of a flower is its only protection against insects."

Read This; It's Funny!

"Mushrooms always grow in damp places and so they look like umbrellas."

"The alimentary canal is located in the northern part of Indiana."

"The skeleton is what is left after the insides have been taken out and the outsides have been taken off. The purpose of the skeleton is something to hitch meat to."

"A permanent set of teeth consists of eight canines, eight cuspids, two molars, and eight cuspidors."

"The tides are a fight between the Earth and moon. All water tends towards the moon, because there is no water in the moon, and nature abhors a vacuum. I forget where the sun joins in this fight."

"A fossil is an extinct animal. The older it is, the more extinct it is."

"Many women believe that an alcoholic binge will have no ill effects on the unborn fetus, but that is a large misconception."

"Equator: A managerie lion running around the Earth through Africa."

"Germinate: To become a naturalized German."

"Liter: A nest of young puppies."

"Magnet: Something you find crawling all over a dead cat."

"Momentum: What you give a person when they are going away."

"Planet: A body of Earth surrounded by sky."

"Rhubarb: A kind of celery gone bloodshot."

"Vacumm: A large, empty space where the pope lives."

"Before giving a blood transfusion, find out if the blood is affirmative or negative."

"To remove dust from the eye, pull the eye down over the nose."

"For a nosebleed: Put the nose much lower than the body until the heart stops."

"For drowning: Climb on top of the person and move up and down to make artifical perspiration."

"For fainting: Rub the person's chest or, if a lady, rub her arm above the hand instead. Or put the head between the knees of the nearest medical doctor."

"For dog bite: put the dog away for several days. If he has not recovered, then kill it."

"For asphyxiation: Apply artificial respiration until the patient is dead."

"To prevent contraception: wear a condominium."

"For head cold: use an agonizer to spray the nose until it drops in your throat."

"To keep milk from turning sour: Keep it in the cow."

Read This; It's Funny!

Subject: Really Awfully Bad Writing

The Worst Analogies
(taken from actual high school papers)

From the attic came an unearthly howl. The whole scene had an eerie, surreal quality, like when you're on vacation in another city and "Jeopardy" comes on at 7 pm instead of 7:30.

The little boat gently drifted across the pond exactly the way a bowling ball wouldn't.

McBride fell 12 stories, hitting the pavement like a Hefty Bag filled with vegetable soup.

Her eyes were like two brown circles with big black dots in the center.

Her vocabulary was as bad as, like, whatever.

He was as tall as a six-foot-three-inch tree.

Long separated by cruel fate, the star-crossed lovers raced across the grassy field toward each other like two freight trains, one having left Cleveland at 6:36 pm traveling at 55 mph, the other from Topeka at 4:19 pm at a speed of 35 mph.

The politician was gone but unnoticed, like the period after the Dr. on a Dr Pepper can.

John and Mary had never met. They were like two hummingbirds who had also never met.

The red brick wall was the color of a brick-red Crayola crayon.

Is It That Time Already?

Subject: The Night Before Thanksgiving 24
Subject: Merry Christmas, Legally Speaking 26
Subject: A Christmas Poem 27
Subject: The Month After Christmas 29
Subject: 12 Days of Christmas................................. 30
Subject: I Think Santa Claus is a Woman.... 35
Subject: Santa and the Angel 37
Subject: Santa's New Contract 38
Subject: Thanksgiving Weather 40
Subject: What Moms REALLY Want 41

Read This; It's Funny!!

Subject: The Night Before Thanksgiving

'Twas the night before Thanksgiving
and all through the kitchen;
I was cooking and baking
and moanin' and bitchin'.
I've been here for hours,
I can't stop to rest,
This place is a disaster,
just look at this mess!

Tomorrow I've got thirty people to feed,
They expect all the trimmings...
who cares what I need!
My feet are both blistered,
I've got cramps in my legs,
The dog just knocked over a bowl full of eggs.

There's a knock at the door
and the telephone's ringing;
Frosting drips on the counter
as the microwave's dinging.
Two pies in the oven,
dessert's almost done;
My cookbook is soiled
with butter and crumbs.

I've had all I can stand,
I can't take anymore;
Then walks in my husband,
spilling rum on the floor.
He heaves and he wobbles,
his balance unsteady;
Then grins as he chuckles
"The eggnog is ready!"
He looks all around
and with total regret,
Says "What's takin' so long?
Aren't you through in here yet??"

Is It That Time Already?

As quick as a flash
I reach for a knife;
He loses an earlobe;
I wanted his life!
He flees from the room
in terror and pain,
and screams "MY GOD WOMAN,
YOU'RE GOING INSANE!!"
Now what was I doing,
and what is that smell?
Oh, great, it's the pies!!
They're burned all to hell!!

I hate to admit
when I make a mistake,
But I put them on BROIL
instead of on BAKE.
What else can go wrong??
Is there still more ahead??
If this is good living,
I'd rather be dead.

Now, don't get me wrong,
I love holidays;
They just leave me exhausted,
all shaky and dazed.
But I promise you one thing,
If I live 'til next year,
You won't find me
pulling my hair out in here.
I'll hire a maid,
a cook, and a waiter;
And if that doesn't work,
I'LL HAVE IT ALL CATERED!

Read This; It's Funny!!

Subject: Merry Christmas, Legally Speaking

Please accept with no obligation, implied or implicit my best wishes for an environmentally conscious, socially responsible, low stress, non-addictive, gender neutral, celebration of the winter solstice holiday, practiced within the most enjoyable traditions of the religious persuasion of your choice, or secular practices of your choice, with respect for the religious/secular persuasions and/or traditions of others, or their choice not to practice religious or secular traditions at all . . .and a fiscally successful, personally fulfilling, and medically uncomplicated recognition of the onset of the generally accepted calendar year 1999, but not without due respect for the calendars of choice of other cultures whose contributions to society have helped make America great, (not to imply that America is necessarily greater than any other country or is the only "AMERICA" in the western hemisphere), and without regard to the race, creed, color, age, physical ability, religious faith, choice of computer platform, or sexual preference of the wishee.

(By accepting this greeting, you are accepting these terms. This greeting is subject to clarification or withdrawal. It is freely transferable with no alteration to the original greeting. It implies no promise by the wisher to actually implement any of the wishes for her/himself or others, and is void where prohibited by law, and is revocable at the sole discretion of the wisher. This wish is warranted to perform as expected within the usual application of good tidings for a period of one year, or until the issuance of a subsequent holiday greeting, whichever comes first, and warranty is limited to replacement of this wish or issuance of a new wish at the sole discretion of the wisher.)

Subject: A Christmas Poem

'Twas the night before Christmas and Santa's a wreck,
How to live in a world that's Politically Correct?
His workers would no longer answer to "Elves".
"Vertically Challenged" they were calling themselves.
And labor conditions at the North Pole,
Were alleged by the union to stifle the soul.

Four reindeer had vanished without much propriety,
Released to the wild by the Humane Society.
And equal employment had made it quite clear,
That Santa had better not use just reindeer.
So Dancer and Donner, Comet and Cupid
Were replaced with four pigs - and did that look stupid!

The runners had been removed from his sleigh;
The ruts were deemed dangerous by the E.P.A.
And people had started to call the cops,
When they heard sled noises on their rooftops.
The secondhand pipe smoke had his workers quite frightened,
And his fur-trimmed suit was called "Unenlightened".

And to show you the strangeness of life's ebbs and flows,
Rudolph was suing over unauthorized use of his nose.
And had gone on Geraldo in front of the whole nation,
Demanding millions in overdue compensation.
And as for the gifts, why he'd never had a notion,
That making a choice could cause so much commotion.

Nothing of leather, nothing of fur,
Which meant nothing for him and nothing for her.
Nothing that might be construed to pollute.
Nothing to aim. Nothing to shoot.
Nothing that clamored or made lots of noise.
Nothing for just girls or just for the boys.

Read This; It's Funny!!

Nothing that claimed to be gender specific.
Nothing that's warlike or non-pacifist.
No candy or sweets.... they were bad for the tooth.
Nothing that seemed to embellish a truth.
And fairy tales, while not yet forbidden,
Were like Ken and Barbie - better off hidden.

For they raised the hackles of those psychological,
Who claimed the only good gift was one ecological.
No baseball, no football.....someone could get hurt.
Besides, playing sports exposed kids to dirt.
Dolls were said to be sexist and should be passe',
And Nintendo would rot your entire brain away.

So Santa just stood there, disheveled and perplexed;
He just could not figure out what to do next.
He tried to be merry, tried to be gay,
But you've got to be careful with that word today.
His sack was quite empty, limp to the ground;
Nothing fully acceptable could be found.

Something special was needed, a gift that he might
Give to all without angering the Left or the Right.
A gift that would satisfy with no indecision,
Each group of people, every religion.
Every ethnicity , every hue,
Everyone everywhere....even you.

So here is the gift, it's price beyond worth,
May you and your loved ones enjoy Peace on Earth !!

Subject: The Month After Christmas

Twas the month after Christmas, and all through the house
Nothing would fit me, not even a blouse.
The cookies I'd nibbled, the eggnog I'd taste
At the holiday parties had gone to my waist.
When I got on the scales there arose such a number!
When I walked to the store (less a walk than a lumber).
I'd remember the marvelous meals I'd prepared;
The gravies and sauces and beef nicely rared,
The wine and the rum balls, the bread and the cheese
And the way I'd never said, "No thank you, please."
As I dressed myself in my husband's old shirt
And prepared once again to do battle with dirt—
I said to myself, as I only can
"You can't spend a winter disguised as a man!"
So—away with the last of the sour cream dip,
Get rid of the fruit cake, every cracker and chip
Every last bit of food that I like must be banished
"Till all the additional ounces have vanished.
I won't have a cookie—not even a lick.
I'll want only to chew on a long celery stick.
I won't have hot biscuits, or corn bread, or pie,
I'll munch on a carrot and quietly cry.
I'm hungry, I'm lonesome, and life is a bore—
But isn't that what January is for?
Unable to giggle, no longer a riot.
Happy New Year to all and to all a good diet!

Read This; It's Funny!!

Subject: 12 Days of Christmas

Miss Sara Truelove
Somewhere, USA

December 26

Dearest Bill:
    I went to the door today and the postman delivered a partridge in a pear tree. What a wonderful thoughtful gift! I couldn't have been more surprised.

With deepest Love and Devotion,
Sara

Miss Sara Truelove
Somewhere, USA

December 27

Dearest Bill:
    Today the postman brought your most wonderful gift. Just imagine - two turtle doves! I'm delighted at your very sweet gift. They are just adorable. I will have to get a cage for them.

With deepest Love,
Sara

Miss Sara Truelove
Somewhere, USA

December 28

Dearest Bill:
    Oh! Your third gift arrived! You really went too far, I think. I don't deserve such generosity - three French hens. They are just lovely, but I must protest - you've been way too kind.

Love,
Sara

Miss Sara Truelove
Somewhere, USA

December 29

Dearest Bill:
    Today the postman delivered four calling birds. Now, really, they're quite nice, but now I have 10 birds and nowhere to put any more.... so please, no more birds!! But, thanks.

Affectionately,
Sara

Miss Sara Truelove
Somewhere, USA

December 30

Dearest Bill:
    What a surprise! Another present.... and not a bird this time! Wow! Today the postman delivered five golden rings, one for each finger. You're just too extravagant, but I love it! Frankly, all those birds squawking were beginning to get on my nerves, but the rings are wonderful... and so quiet!!

All my love,
Sara

Miss Sara Truelove
Somewhere, USA

December 31

Dear Bill:
    When I opened the door there were actually six geese a-laying on my front steps. So you're back to the birds again, huh? Those geese are huge! And it was bird poop that they were laying.. complete with a large count of coloform bacteria. Where will I ever keep them? The neighbors are complaining. The police came by with a formal complaint, and I can't sleep through all the racket. I guess I have my own noisemakers for the New Year's Eve celebration tonight.

Read This; It's Funny!!

Please stop. NO MORE BIRDS!!

Cordially,
Sara

Miss Sara Truelove
Somewhere, USA

January 1

Bill:
Happy New Year... to some people. It hasn't been so happy
with me. What's with you and those dumb birds? Seven swans
a-swimming. What kind of practical joke is this? There's bird
guano all over the house and they never stop squawking. I could
not sleep all night and I'm a nervous wreck. You have gone too
far, bird brain. STOP SENDING BIRDS. NO MORE BIRDS!!
GOT IT?

Sincerely,
Sara

Miss Sara Truelove
Somewhere, USA

January 2

OK, WISE GUY:
I think I prefer the birds over this. What am I going to do
with eight maids a-milking? It's not enough with all those birds
and eight maids a-milking, but they had to bring their cows.
Have you ever smelled a yard full of cow patties? Their piles are
all over the lawn, and I can't move in my own house. Leave me
alone. NO MORE OF YOUR "GIFTS".

Sara

Miss Sara Truelove
Somewhere, USA

January 3

Hey, Vacuum-for-a-brain:

What are you? Some kind of freak? Now there's nine ladies dancing... right in the smelly you-know-what and tracking it all over my house. The way they've been bickering with the milk maids, I hesitate to even call them ladies. You'll get yours, buddy.

Sara

Miss Sara Truelove
Somewhere, USA

January 4

You rotten piece of cow patty:

What's with the ten lords a-leaping? I have threatened to break their legs so that they can never leap again. All 23 of the birds are dead. They've been trampled to death by the leapers, the dancers, and the cows. At least, I don't have to worry about them any more. However, the cows are mooing all night having gotten diarrhea. My living room is a sewer! The City Commissioner has subpoenaed me to give cause why my house shouldn't be condemned.

I'm filing a complaint to the police about you!

One who means it.

Miss Sara Truelove
Somewhere, USA

January 5

Listen, brainless:

Now there's eleven pipers piping. And they never stop piping... except when they're chasing those maids or dancing girls. The cows are getting very upset and are sounding worse than the birds ever did. What am I going to do? There is a petition going around to evict me from the neighborhood.

I hope you're satisfied, you rotten, vicious swine.

Your sworn enemy,
Sara

Read This; It's Funny!!

Law Offices
Sue, Pillage, and Plunder
1313 Grunge St
Somewhere, USA

January 6

Dear Sir:

This is to acknowledge your latest gift of twelve drummers drumming which you have seen fit to inflict on our client, Miss Sara Truelove. The damage, of course, was total. She was found beating her head against the wall to the beat of the twelve drums. If you should attempt to reach Miss Truelove at Happy Glen Sanitarium, the attendants have instructions to shoot you on sight. With this letter, please find attached a warrant for your arrest.

Cordially,
Law Firm of Sue, Pillage, and Plunder

Subject: I Think Santa Claus is a Woman....

I hate to be the one to defy sacred myth, but I believe he's a she.

Think about it. Christmas is a big, organized, warm, fuzzy, nurturing social deal, and I have a tough time believing a guy could possibly pull it all off!

For starters, the vast majority of men don't even think about selecting gifts until Christmas Eve. It's as if they are all frozen in some kind of Ebenezerian Time Warp until 3 p.m. on Dec. 24th, when they - with amazing calm - call other errant men and plan for a last-minute shopping spree.

Once at the mall, they always seem surprised to find only Ronco products, socket wrench sets, and mood rings left on the shelves. (You might think this would send them into a fit of panic and guilt, but my husband tells me it's an enormous relief because it lessens the 11th hour decision-making burden.)

On this count alone, I'm convinced Santa is a woman.

Surely, if he were a man, everyone in the universe would wake up Christmas morning to find a rotating musical Chia Pet under the tree, still in the bag.

Another problem for a he-Santa would be getting there. First of all, there would be no reindeer because they would all be dead, gutted and strapped on to the rear bumper of the sleigh amid wide-eyed, desperate claims that buck season had been extended. Blitzen's rack would already be on the way to the taxidermist.

Even if the male Santa DID have reindeer, he'd still have transportation problems because he would inevitably get lost up there in the snow and clouds and then refuse to stop and ask for directions. Add to this the fact that there would be unavoidable delays in the chimney, where the Bob Vila-like Santa would stop to inspect and repoint bricks in the flue. He would also need to check for carbon monoxide fumes in every gas fireplace, and get under every Christmas tree that is crooked to straighten it to a perfectly upright 90-degree angle.

Other reasons why Santa can't possibly be a man:

- Men can't pack a bag.
- Men would rather be dead than caught wearing red velvet.
- Men would feel their masculinity is threatened... having to be seen with all those elves.
- Men don't answer their mail.

35

Read This; It's Funny!!

- Men would refuse to allow their physique to be described even in jest as anything remotely resembling a "bowlful of jelly."

- Men aren't interested in stockings unless somebody's wearing them.

- Having to do the Ho Ho Ho thing would seriously inhibit their ability to pick up women.

- Finally, being responsible for Christmas would require a commitment.

I can buy the fact that other mythical holiday characters are men.........

Father Time shows up once a year unshaven and looking ominous.

Definite guy.

Cupid flies around carrying weapons. Uncle Sam is a politician who likes to point fingers. Any one of these individuals could pass the testosterone screening test. But not St. Nick. Not a chance.

As long as we have each other, good will, peace on earth, faith and Nat King Cole's version of "The Christmas Song," it probably makes little difference what gender Santa is.

I just wish she'd quit dressing like a man.

Subject: Santa and the Angel

Not long ago and far away, Santa was getting ready for his annual trip... but there were problems everywhere. Four of his elves got sick, and the trainee elves did not produce the toys as fast as the regular ones so Santa was beginning to feel the pressure of being behind schedule.

Then Mrs. Claus told Santa that her Mom was coming to visit. This stressed Santa even more. When he went to harness the reindeer, he found that three of them were about to give birth and two had jumped the fence and were out, heaven knows where to. More Stress!

Then when he began to load the sleigh, one of the boards cracked and the toy bag fell to the ground and scattered the toys. Totally frustrated, Santa went into the house for a cup of coffee and a shot of whiskey. When he went to the cupboard, he found the elves had hit the liquor and there was nothing to drink. In his frustration, he dropped the coffee pot and it broke into hundreds of little pieces all over the kitchen floor.

He went to get the broom and found that mice had eaten the straw it was made from.

Just then the doorbell rang and Santa cussed on his way to the door. He opened the door and there was a little angel with a great big Christmas tree. The angel said: "Where would you like to put this tree, fat man?"

And that, my friend, is how the little angel came to be on top of the Christmas tree.

Read This; It's Funny!!

Subject: Santa's New Contract

I regret to inform you that, effective immediately, I will no longer be able to serve Southern United States on Christmas Eve. Due to the overwhelming current population of the earth, my contract was renegotiated by North American Fairies and Elves Local 269. I now serve only certain areas of Ohio, Indiana, Illinois, Wisconsin and Michigan. As part of the new and better contract I also get longer breaks for milk and cookies so keep that in mind. However, I'm certain your children will be in good hands with your local replacement who happens to be my third cousin, Bubba Claus.

His side of the family is from the South Pole. He shares my goal of delivering toys to all the good boys and girls; however, there are a few differences between us.

1. There is no danger of a Grinch stealing your presents from Bubba Claus.

He has a gun rack on his sleigh and a bumper sticker that reads: "These toys insured by Smith and Wesson."

2. Instead of milk and cookies, Bubba Claus prefers that children leave an RC cola and pork rinds [or a moon pie] on the fireplace. And Bubba doesn't smoke a pipe. He dips a little snuff though, so please have an empty spit cup handy.

3. Bubba Claus' sleigh is pulled by floppy-eared, flyin' coon dogs instead of reindeer.

I made the mistake of loaning him a couple of my reindeer one time, and Blitzen's head now overlooks Bubba's fireplace.

4. You won't hear "On Comet, on Cupid, on Donner and Blitzen ..." when Bubba Claus arrives. Instead, you'll hear, "On Earnhardt, on Wallace, on Martin and Labonte. On Rudd, on Jarrett, on Elliott and Petty."

5. "Ho, ho, ho!" has been replaced by "Yee Haw!" And you also are likely to hear Bubba's elves respond, "I her'd dat!"

6. As required by Southern highway laws, Bubba Claus' sleigh does have a Yosemite Sam safety triangle on the back with the words "Back off". The last I heard it also had other decorations on the sleigh back as well.

One is a Ford or Chevy logo with lights that race through the letters and the other is a caricature of me (Santa Claus) going wee wee on the Tooth Fairy.

7. The usual Christmas movie classics such as "Miracle on 34th Street" and "It's a Wonderful Life" will not be shown in your

negotiated viewing area.

Instead, you'll see "Boss Hogg Saves Christmas" and "Smokey and the Bandit IV" featuring Burt Reynolds as Bubba Claus and dozens of state patrol cars crashing into each other.
8. Bubba Claus doesn't wear a belt. If I were you, I'd make sure you, the wife, and the kids turn the other way when he bends over to put presents under the tree.
9. And finally, lovely Christmas songs have been sung about me like "Rudolph The Red-nosed Reindeer" and Bing Crosby's "Santa Claus Is Coming to Town." This year songs about Bubba Claus will be played on all the AM radio stations in the South. Those song titles will be Mark Chesnutt's "Bubba Claus Shot the Jukebox" and "Grandma Got Run'd Over by a Reindeer."

Sincerely Yours,

Santa Claus (member of North American Fairies and Elves Local 209)

Read This; It's Funny!!

Subject: Thanksgiving Weather

Turkeys will thaw in the morning, then warm in the oven to an afternoon high near 190°F. The kitchen will turn hot and humid, and if you bother the cook, be ready for a severe squall or cold shoulder.

During the late afternoon and evening, the cold front of a knife will slice through the turkey, causing an accumulation of one to two inches on plates. Mashed potatoes will drift across one side while cranberry sauce creates slippery spots on the other. Please pass the gravy.

A weight watch and indigestion warning have been issued for the entire area, with increased stuffiness around the beltway. During the evening, the turkey will diminish and taper off to leftovers, dropping to a low of 34°F in the refrigerator.

Looking ahead to Friday and Saturday, high pressure to eat sandwiches will be established. Flurries of leftovers can be expected both days with a 50 percent chance of scattered soup late in the day. We expect a warming trend where soup develops. By early next week, eating pressure will be low as the only wish left will be the bone.

Happy Thanksgiving!

Subject: What Moms REALLY Want

Top 10 List of what Moms REALLY want for Mother's Day

10. To be able to eat a whole candy bar (alone) and drink a soda without any "floaties" (ie, backwash)
9. To have my 14 year-old daughter answer a question without rolling her eyes in that "Why is this person my mother?" way.
8. Five pounds of chocolate that won't add twenty.
7. A shower without a child peeking through the curtain with a "Hi Ya Mom!" just as I put a razor to my ankle.
6. A full time cleaning person who looks like Brad Pitt.
5. For my teenager to announce "Hey, Mom! I got a full scholarship and a job all in the same day!"
4. A grocery store that doesn't have candy/gum/cheap toys displayed at the checkout line.
3. To have a family meal without a discussion about bodily secretions.
2. To be able to step on a plane with my toddlers and NOT have someone moan, "Oh no! Why me...!"

And the #1 thing that moms REALLY want for Mother's Day is.....

Four words: Fisher Price Play Prison

Family

Subject: Before Children/After Children 43
Subject: Cost of Kids 45
Subject: Just a Mother 47
Subject: Lesson for the Day 49
Subject: Mustard 50
Subject: Potty Humor 51
Subject: Somebody Said 52
Subject: Things Your Mother Wouldn't Say 54
Subject: Why Parents Have Gray Hair 55
Subject: Christmas Intent 56

Subject: Before Children/After Children

BEFORE CHILDREN: I was thankful to have been born in the USA, the most powerful free democracy in the world.
AFTER CHILDREN : I am thankful for Velcro tennis shoes. As well as saving valuable time, now I can hear the sound of my son taking off his shoes — which gives me three extra seconds to activate the safety locks on the back seat windows right before he hurls them out of the car and onto the freeway.

BEFORE CHILDREN: I was thankful for the recycling program which will preserve our natural resources and prevent the overloading of landfills.
AFTER CHILDREN : I am thankful for swim diapers because every time my son wanders into water in plain disposables, he ends up wearing a blimp the size of, say, New Jersey, on his bottom.

BEFORE CHILDREN: I was thankful for fresh, organic vegetables.
AFTER CHILDREN : I am thankful for microwaveable macaroni and cheese — without which my children would be surviving on about three bites of cereal and their own spit.

BEFORE CHILDREN: I was thankful for the opportunity to obtain a college education and have a higher quality of life than my ancestors.
AFTER CHILDREN : I am thankful to finish a complete thought without being interrupted.

BEFORE CHILDREN: I was thankful for holistic medicine and natural herbs.
AFTER CHILDREN : I am thankful for pediatric cough syrup guaranteed to "cause drowsiness"; in young children.

BEFORE CHILDREN: I was thankful for all of the teachers who had taught, encouraged and nurtured me throughout my formative years.
AFTER CHILDREN : I am thankful for all of the people at Weight Watcher who let me strip down to pantyhose and a strategically placed scarf before getting on the scale each week.

Read This; It's Funny!!

BEFORE CHILDREN: I was thankful for the opportunity to vacation in exotic foreign countries so I could experience a different way of life in a new culture.
AFTER CHILDREN : I am thankful to have time to make it all the way down the driveway to get the mail.

BEFORE CHILDREN: I was thankful for the Moosewood Vegetarian cookbook.
AFTER CHILDREN : I am thankful for the butterball turkey hotline.

BEFORE CHILDREN: I was thankful for a warm, cozy home to share with my loved ones.
AFTER CHILDREN : I am thankful for the lock on the bathroom door.

BEFORE CHILDREN: I was thankful for material objects like custom furniture, a nice car and trendy clothes.
AFTER CHILDREN : I am thankful when the baby spits up and misses my good shoes.

BEFORE CHILDREN: I was thankful for my wonderful family
AFTER CHILDREN : I am thankful for my wonderful family.

Subject: Cost of Kids

The government recently calculated the cost of raising a child from birth to 18 and came up with $160,140 for a middle income family. Talk about sticker shock! That doesn't even touch college tuition. But $160,140 isn't so bad if you break it down. It translates into $8,896.66 a year, $741.38 a month, or $171.08 a week. That's a mere $24.24 a day! Just over a dollar an hour.

Still, you might think the best financial advice says don't have children if you want to be "rich." It is just the opposite. What do you get for your $160,140?

Naming rights. First, middle, and last!

Glimpses of God every day.

Giggles under the covers every night.

More love than your heart can hold.

Butterfly kisses and Velcro hugs.

Endless wonder over rocks, ants, clouds, and warm cookies.

A hand to hold, usually covered with jam.

A partner for blowing bubbles, flying kites, building sandcastles, and skipping down the sidewalk in the pouring rain.

Someone to laugh yourself silly with no matter what the boss said or how your stocks performed that day.

For $160,140, you never have to grow up.

You get to finger-paint, carve pumpkins, play hide-and-seek, catch lightning bugs, and never stop believing in Santa Claus.

You have an excuse to keep: reading the Adventures of Piglet and Pooh, watching Saturday morning cartoons, going to Disney movies, and wishing on stars.

You get to frame rainbows, hearts, and flowers under refrigerator magnets and collect spray painted noodle wreaths for Christmas, hand prints set in clay for Mother's Day, and cards with backward letters for Father's Day.

For $160,140, there is no greater bang for your buck.

You get to be a hero just for retrieving a Frisbee off the garage roof, taking the training wheels off the bike, removing a splinter, filling a wading pool, coaxing a wad of gum out of bangs, and coaching a baseball team that never wins but always gets treated to ice cream regardless.

You get a front row seat to history to witness the first step, first word, first bra, first date, and first time behind the wheel.

You get to be immortal.

You get another branch added to your family tree, and if

you're lucky, a long list of limbs in your obituary called grandchildren.

You get an education in psychology, nursing, criminal justice, communications, and human sexuality that no college can match.

In the eyes of a child, you rank right up there with God.

You have all the power to heal a boo-boo, scare away the monsters under the bed, patch a broken heart, police a slumber party, ground them forever, and love them without limits, so one day they will, like you, love without counting the cost.

ENJOY YOUR KIDS AND GRANDKIDS.

Subject: Just a Mother

A few months ago, when I was picking up the children at school, another mother I knew well rushed up to me.

Emily was fuming with indignation. "Do you know what you and I are?" she demanded.

Before I could answer and I didn't really have one handy..... she blurted out the reason for her question. It seemed she had just returned from renewing her driver's license at the County Clerk's office. Asked by the woman recorder to state her occupation,

Emily had hesitated, uncertain how to classify herself.

"What I mean is," explained the recorder, "do you have a job, or are you just a...?"

"Of course I have a job," snapped Emily. "I'm a Mother."

"We don't list 'mother' as an occupation...'housewife' covers it," said the recorder emphatically.

I forgot all about her story until one day I found myself in the same situation, this time at our own Town Hall. The Clerk was obviously a career woman, poised, efficient, and possessed of a high-sounding title like "Official Interrogator" or "Town Registrar."

"What is your occupation?" she probed.

What made me say it, I do not know. The words simply popped out. "I am a Research Associate in the field of Child Development and Human Relations."

The clerk paused, ball-point pen frozen in midair, and looked up as though she had not heard right. I repeated the title slowly, emphasizing the most significant words. Then I stared with wonder as my pronouncement was written in bold, black ink on the official questionnaire.

"Might I ask," said the clerk with new interest, "just what you do in your field?"

Coolly, without any trace of fluster in my voice, I heard myself reply, "I have a continuing program of research (what mother doesn't) in the laboratory and in the field (normally I would have said indoors and out). I'm working for my Masters (the whole darned family) and already have four credits (all daughters!). Of course, the job is one of the most demanding in the humanities (any mother care to disagree?) and I often work 14 hours a day (24 is more like it). But the job is more challenging than most run-of-the mill careers and the rewards are more of a satisfaction rather than just money."

There was an increasing note of respect in the clerk's voice as she completed the form, stood up, and personally ushered me to the door.

As I drove into our driveway, buoyed up by my glamorous new career, I was greeted by my lab assistants - ages 13, 7, and 3. Upstairs I could hear our new experimental model (6 months) in the child-development program, testing out a new vocal pattern.

I felt triumphant! I had scored a beat on bureaucracy!

And I had gone on the official records as someone more distinguished and indipensable to mankind than 'just another mother.'

Motherhood...what a glorious career. Especially when there's a title on the door.

Subject: Lesson for the Day

John invited his mother over for dinner. During the meal, his mother couldn't help noticing how beautiful John's roommate was. She had long been suspicious of a relationship between John and his roommate and this only made her more curious.

Over the course of the evening, while watching the two interact, she started to wonder if there was more between John and the roommate than met the eye.

Reading his mom's thoughts, John volunteered, "I know what you must be thinking, but I assure you, Julie and I are just roommates."

About a week later, Julie came to John and said, "Ever since your mother came to dinner, I've been unable to find the beautiful silver gravy ladle.

You don't think she took it, do you?" John said, "Well, I doubt it, but I'll write her a letter just to be sure." So he sat down and wrote:

"Dear Mother,
I'm not saying you 'did' take a gravy ladle from my house, and I'm not saying you 'did not' take a gravy ladle. But the fact remains that one has been missing ever since you were here for dinner."

Several days later, John received a letter from his mother which read:

"Dear Son,
I'm not saying that you 'do' sleep with Julie, and I'm not saying that you 'do not' sleep with Julie. But the fact remains that if she was sleeping in her own bed, she would have found the gravy ladle by now.
Love, Mom"

Lesson for the day ... Don't lie to your mother.

Read This; It's Funny!!

Subject: Mustard

As ham sandwiches go, it was perfection. A thick slab of ham, a fresh bun, crisp lettuce and plenty of expensive, light brown, gourmet mustard. The corners of my jaw aching in anticipation, I carried it to the table in our backyard, picked it up with both hands but was stopped by my wife suddenly at my side. "Hold Johnny (our six week-old son) while I get my sandwich," she said.

I had him balanced between my left elbow and shoulder and was reaching again for the ham sandwich when I noticed a streak of mustard on my fingers.

I love mustard. I had no napkin. I licked it off.

It was not mustard. No man ever put a baby down faster. It was the first and only time I have sprinted with my tongue protruding. With a washcloth in each hand I did the sort of routine shoeshine boys do, only I did it on my tongue.

Later (after she stopped crying from laughing so hard) my wife said, "Now you know why they call that mustard 'Poupon'."

Subject: Potty Humor

My three year old son had a lot of problems with potty training; and I was on him constantly. One day we stopped at Taco Bell for a quick lunch in between errands. It was very busy, with a full dining room.

While enjoying my taco, I smelled something funny, so of course, I checked my seven month old daughter, and she was clean.

Then I realized that Matt had not asked to go potty in a while, so I asked him and he said, "No."

I kept thinking, "Oh Lord, that child has had an accident and I didn't have any clothes with me."

Then I said, "Matt, are you sure you did not have an accident?"

"No," he replied. I just knew that he must have, because the smell was getting worse. Sooooo.... I asked one more time, "Matt, did you have an accident?"

Matt jumped up, yanked down his pants, bent over and spread his cheeks and yelled.... "SEE, MOM, IT'S JUST FARTS!!!"

While 100 people nearly choked to death on their tacos, he calmly pulled up his pants and sat down to eat his food as if nothing happened. I was mortified!

Some kind elderly people made me feel a lot better, when they came over and thanked me for the best laugh they had ever had!!!

Another old gentleman stopped us in the parking lot as we were leaving, bent over to my son and said, "Don't worry son, my wife accuses me of the same thing all the time...I just never had the nerve to make the point like you did."

Read This; It's Funny!!

Subject: Somebody Said

Somebody said it takes about six weeks to get back to normal after you've had a baby
...somebody doesn't know that once you're a mother, "normal" is history.

Somebody said a mother's job consists of wiping noses and changing diapers
...somebody doesn't know that a child is much more than the shell he lives in.

Somebody said you learn how to be a mother by instinct
...somebody never took a three-year-old shopping.

Somebody said being a mother is boring
...somebody never rode in a car driven by a teenager with a driver's permit.

Somebody said teachers, psychologists and pediatricians know more about children than their mothers
...somebody hasn't invested her heart in another human being.

Somebody said if you're a "good" mother, your child will "turn out"
...somebody thinks a child is like a bag of plaster of Paris that comes with directions, a mold and a guarantee.

Somebody said being a mother is what you do in your spare time
...somebody doesn't know that when you're a mother, you're a mother ALL the time.

Somebody said "good" mothers never raise their voices
...somebody never came out the back door just in time to see her child wind up and hit a golf ball through the neighbor's kitchen window.

Somebody said the hardest part of being a mother is labor and delivery
...somebody never watched her "baby" get on the bus for the first day of kindergarten.

52

Somebody said you don't need an education to be a mother
...somebody never helped a fourth grader with his math.

Somebody said you can't love the fifth child as much as you love the first
...somebody doesn't have five children.

Somebody said a mother can find all the answers to her child-rearing questions in the books
...somebody never had a child stuff beans up his nose.

Somebody said a mother can do her job with her eyes closed and one hand tied behind her back
...somebody never organized seven giggling Brownies to sell cookies.

Somebody said a mother can stop worrying after her child gets married
...somebody doesn't know that marriage adds a new son or daughter-in-law to a mother's heartstrings.

Somebody said a mother's job is done when her last child leaves home
...somebody never had grandchildren.

Somebody said being a mother is a side dish on the plate of life
...somebody doesn't know what fills you up.

Somebody said your mother knows you love her, so you don't need to tell her
...somebody isn't a mother.

Pass this along to all the "mothers" in your life.

Read This; It's Funny!!

Subject: Things Your Mother Wouldn't Say

"Be good and for your birthday I'll buy you a motorcycle!"

"How on earth can you see the TV sitting so far back?"

"Don't bother wearing a jacket—it's quite warm out."

"Let me smell that shirt—yeah, it's good for another week."

"I think a cluttered bedroom is a sign of creativity."

"Yeah, I used to skip school, too."

"Just leave all the lights on...it makes the house more cheery."

"Could you turn the music up louder so I can enjoy it, too?"

"Run and bring me the scissors! Hurry!"

"Aw, just turn these undies inside out. No one will ever know."

"I don't have a tissue with me—just use your sleeve."

"Well, if Timmy's Mom says it's okay, that's good enough for me."

"Of course you should walk to school and back. What's the big deal about having to cross a few main streets?"

"My meeting won't be over till later tonight. You kids don't mind if we skip dinner?"

Subject: Why Parents Have Gray Hair

The boss of a big company needed to call one of his employees about an urgent problem with one of the main computers.

He dialed the employee's home phone number and was greeted with a child's whispered, "Hello?"

Feeling put out at the inconvenience of having to talk to a youngster, the boss asked, "Is your Daddy home?"

"Yes," whispered the small voice.

"May I talk with him?" the man asked.

To the surprise of the boss, the small voice whispered, "No."

Wanting to talk with an adult, the boss asked, "Is your Mommy there?"

"Yes," came the answer.

"May I talk with her?"

Again the small voice whispered, "No."

Knowing that it was not likely that a young child would be left home alone, the boss decided he would just leave a message with the person who should be there watching over the child. "Is there anyone else there in your house?" the boss asked the child.

"Yes," whispered the child, "a policeman."

Wondering what a cop would be doing at his employee's home, the Boss asked, "May I speak with the policeman?"

"No, he's busy," whispered the child.

"Busy doing what?" asked the boss.

"Talking to Daddy and Mommy and the fireman," whispered the child.

Growing concerned and even worried as he heard what sounded like a helicopter through the earpiece on the phone, the boss asked, "What is that noise?"

"A hello-copper," answered the whispering voice.

"What is going on there?" asked the boss, now alarmed.

In an awed hushed voice the child answered, "The search team just landed the hello-copper."

Alarmed, concerned and more than just a little frustrated, the boss asked, "What are they searching for?"

Still whispering, the young voice replied, along with a muffled giggle: "Me."

Read This; It's Funny!!

Subject: Christmas Intent

A man in Phoenix calls his son in New York the day before Christmas and says, "I hate to ruin your day, but I have to tell you that your Mom and I are divorcing; forty-five years of misery is enough."

"Pop, what are you talking about?" the son screams.

"We can't stand the sight of each other any longer," the father says. "We're sick of each other, and I'm sick of talking about this, so you call your sister in Chicago and tell her."

Frantic, the son calls his sister, who explodes on the phone.

"Like heck they're getting divorced," she shouts, "I'll take care of this," She calls Phoenix immediately, and screams at her father, "You are NOT getting divorced. Don't do a single thing until I get there. I'm calling my brother back, and we'll both be there tomorrow. Until then, don't do a thing, DO YOU HEAR ME?" and hangs up.

The old man hangs up his phone and turns to his wife. "Okay," he says, "they're coming for Christmas and paying their own way."

Take Action

Subject: Deteriorata 58
Subject: Instructions for Life 60
Subject: Try This 62

Read This; It's Funny!!

Subject: Deteriorata

Go placidly
Amid the noise and waste.
And remember what comfort there may be
In owning a piece thereof.

Avoid quiet and passive persons
Unless you are in need of sleep.

Rotate your tires.

Speak glowingly of those greater than yourself
And heed well their advice,
Even though they be turkeys.

Know what to kiss.....and when!

Consider that two wrongs never make a right
But that THREE.........do.

Wherever possible, put people on hold.

Be comforted that in the face of all aridity and disillusionment
And despite the changing fortunes of time,
There is always a big future in computer maintenance.

Remember the Pueblo.

Strive at all times to bend, fold, spindle and mutilate.

Know yourself.
If you need help, call the FBI.

Exercise caution in your daily affairs,
Especially with those persons closest to you.
That lemon on your left, for instance.

Be assured that a walk through the ocean of most souls
Would scarcely get your feet wet.

Fall not in love therefore;
It will stick to your face.

Gracefully surrender the things of youth:
The birds, clean air, tuna, Taiwan
And let not the sands of time
Get in your lunch.

Hire people with hooks.

For a good time call 555-555-4311;
Ask for "Ken."

Take heart amid the deepening gloom
That your dog is finally getting enough cheese.

And reflect that whatever misfortune may be your lot
It could only be worse in Milwaukee.

Therefore, make peace with your god
Whatever you conceive him to be—
Hairy thunderer, or cosmic muffin.

With all its hopes, dreams, promises and urban renewal
The world continues to deteriorate.

GIVE UP!

You are a fluke
Of the universe.
You have no right to be here.
And whether you can hear it or not
The universe is laughing behind your back.

Read This; It's Funny!!

Subject: Instructions for Life

1. Give people more than they expect and do it cheerfully.
2. Memorize your favorite poem.
3. Don't believe all you hear, spend all you have or sleep all you want.
4. When you say, "I love you", mean it.
5. When you say, "I'm sorry", look the person in the eye.
6. Be engaged at least six months before you get married.
7. Believe in love at first sight.
8. Never laugh at anyone's dreams.
9. Love deeply and passionately. You might get hurt but it's the only way to live life completely.
10. In disagreements, fight fairly. No name calling.
11. Don't judge people by their relatives.
12. Talk slowly but think quickly.
13. When someone asks you a question you don't want to answer, smile and ask, "Why do you want to know?"
14. Remember that great love and great achievements involve great risk.
15. Call your mom.
16. Say "bless you" when you hear someone sneeze.
17. When you lose, don't lose the lesson.
18. Remember the three R's: Respect for self, Respect for others, Responsibility for all your actions.
19. Don't let a little dispute injure a great friendship.
20. When you realize you've made a mistake, take immediate steps to correct it.
21. Smile when picking up the phone. The caller will hear it in your voice.
22. Marry a man/woman you love to talk to. As you get older, their conversational skills will be as important as any other.
23. Spend some time alone.
24. Open your arms to change, but don't let go of your values.
25. Remember that silence is sometimes the best answer.
26. Read more books and watch less TV.
27. Live a good, honorable life. Then when you get older and think back, you'll get to enjoy it a second time.
28. Trust in God but lock your car.
29. A loving atmosphere in your home is so important. Do all you can to create a tranquil harmonious home.
30. Read between the lines.

31. In disagreements with loved ones, deal with the current situation. Don't bring up the past.

32. Share your knowledge. It's a way to achieve immortality.

33. Be gentle with the earth.

34. Pray. There's immeasurable power in it.

35. Never interrupt when you are being flattered.

36. Mind your own business.

37. Don't trust a man/woman who doesn't close his/her eyes when you kiss.

38. Once a year, go someplace you've never been before.

39. If you make a lot of money, put it to use helping others while you are living. That is wealth's greatest satisfaction.

40. Remember that not getting what you want is sometimes a stroke of luck.

41. Learn the rules then break some.

42. Remember that the best relationship is one where your love for each other is greater than your need for each other.

43. Judge your success by what you had to give up in order to get it.

44. Remember that your character is your destiny.

45. Approach love and cooking with reckless abandon.

Read This; It's Funny!!

Subject: Try This

See if you can do this? Read this out loud.

This is this cat
This is is cat
This is how cat
This is to cat
This is keep cat
This is a cat
This is retard cat
This is busy cat
This is for cat
This is forty cat
This is seconds cat

Scroll down .....

Now go back and read the THIRD word, in each line, from the start.

Everyone knows someone they can send THIS too!!!

Signs of the Times

Subject: Bumper Stickers 1 64
Subject: Bumper Stickers 2 67
Subject: Cute Signs 68
Subject: Women's T-Shirts.. 70
Subject: Actual Headlines... 71
Subject: T-Shirt Slogans 72
Subject: Rejected Hallmark Cards 75

Read This; It's Funny!!

Subject: Bumper Stickers 1

So many stupid people... so few comets.

Your kid may be an honors student, but you're still an idiot.

All generalizations are false.

Cover me. I'm changing lanes.

I brake for no apparent reason.

I'm not as think as you drunk I am.

Forget about World Peace...Visualize using your turn signal.

We have enough youth, how about a fountain of Smart?

He who laughs last thinks slowest.

Lottery: A tax on people who are bad at math.

It IS as bad as you think, and they ARE out to get you.

Auntie Em: Hate you, hate Kansas, taking the dog. — Dorothy

Time is what keeps everything from happening at once.

I love cats...they taste just like chicken.

Out of my mind. Back in five minutes.

Born free...Taxed to death.

The more people I meet, the more I like my dog.

Laugh alone and the world thinks you're an idiot.

I get enough exercise just pushing my luck.

Sometimes I wake up grumpy; Other times I let him sleep.

Work is for people who don't know how to fish.

I didn't fight my way to the top of the food chain to be a vegetarian.

Women who seek to be equal to men lack ambition.

If you don't like the news, go out and make some.

When you do a good deed, get a receipt in case heaven is like the IRS.

No Radio - Already Stolen.

Real women don't have hot flashes, they have power surges.

I took an IQ test and the results were negative.

Where there's a will, I want to be in it.

OK, who stopped payment on my reality check?

Few women admit their age: Fewer men act it.

I don't suffer from insanity, I enjoy every minute of it.

Tell me to 'stuff it' - I'm a taxidermist.

IRS: We've got what it takes to take what you've got.

Time is the best teacher. Unfortunately, it kills all its students.

It's lonely at the top, but you eat better.

According to my calculations, the problem doesn't exist.

Some people are only alive because it is illegal to kill.

Pride is what we have. Vanity is what others have.

A bartender is just a pharmacist with a limited inventory.

Read This; It's Funny!!

Reality? Is that where the pizza delivery guy comes from?

Warning: Dates in calendar are closer than they appear.

Give me ambiguity or give me something else.

A woman without a man is like a neck without a pain.

We are born naked, wet, and hungry. Then things get worse.

Make it idiot-proof and someone will make a better idiot.

Always remember you're unique, just like everyone else.

Friends help you move. Real friends help you move bodies.

Very funny, Scotty — now beam down my clothes.

Consciousness: That annoying time between naps.

I souport publik edekashun.

Be nice to your kids. They'll choose your nursing home.

There are three kinds of people: those who can count and those who can't.

Why is 'abbreviation' such a long word?

Ever stop to think and forget to start again?

Keep honking...I'm reloading.

Caution: I drive like you do.

My kid beat up your honor student!

So many cats, so few recipes.

Subject: Bumper Stickers 2

* When everything's coming your way, you're in the wrong lane.

* I couldn't repair your brakes, so I made your horn louder.

* Eagles may soar, but weasels don't get sucked into jet engines.

* The early bird may get the worm, but the second mouse gets the cheese.

* Energizer Bunny arrested; charged with battery.

* Laughing stock: cattle with a sense of humor.

* Everyone has a photographic memory. Some don't have film.

* Change is inevitable, except from a vending machine.

Read This; It's Funny!!

Subject: Cute Signs

Septic tank truck sign reads:
"We're #1 in the #2 business".

Sign over a gynecologist's office:
"Dr. Jones, at your cervix."

At a proctologist's door
"To expedite your visit please back in."

On a plumber's truck:
"We repair what your husband fixed."

On the trucks of a local plumbing company:
"Don't sleep with a drip. Call your plumber."

Pizza shop slogan:
"7 days without pizza makes one weak."

At a tire shop in Milwaukee:
"Invite us to your next blowout."

Door of a plastic surgeon's office:
"Hello. Can we pick your nose?"

At a laundry shop:
"How about we refund your money, send you a new one at no charge, close the store and have the manager shot. Would that be satisfactory?"

At a towing company:
"We don't charge an arm and a leg. We want tows."

On an electrician's truck:
"Let us remove your shorts."

On a maternity room door:
 "Push. Push. Push."

In a podiatrist's office:
"Time wounds all heels."

68

In a nonsmoking area:
"If we see smoke, we will assume you are on fire and take appropriate action."

At an optometrist's office:
"If you don't see what you're looking for, you've come to the right place."

On a taxidermist's window:
"We really know our stuff."

On a fence:
"Salesmen welcome! Dog food is expensive."

At a car dealership:
"The best way to get back on your feet - miss a car payment."

Outside a muffler shop:
"No appointment necessary. We hear you coming."

In a veterinarian's waiting room:
"Be back in 5 minutes. Sit! Stay!"

At the electric company:
"We would be delighted if you send in your bill. However, if you don't, you will be."

In a restaurant window:
"Don't stand there and be hungry .. Come on in and get fed up."

In the front yard of a funeral home:
"Drive carefully. We'll wait."

At a propane filling station,
"Tank heaven for little grills."

And don't forget the sign at a Chicago radiator shop:
 "Best place in town to take a leak."

Read This; It's Funny!!

Subject: Women's T-Shirts

Don't tick me off! I'm running out of places to hide the bodies.

Guys have feelings too. But like... who cares?

I don't believe in miracles. I rely on them.

Next mood swing: 6 minutes.

I hate everybody, and you're next.

Please don't make me kill you.

And your point is...

I used to be schizophrenic, but we're OK now.

I'm busy. You're ugly. Have a nice day.

Warning: I have an attitude and I know how to use it.

Of course I don't look busy... I did it right the first time.

Why do people with closed minds always open their mouths?

I'm multi-talented: I can talk and tick you off at the same time.

Do NOT start with me. You will NOT win.

You have the right to remain silent, so please SHUT UP.

All stressed out and no one to choke.

I'm one of those bad things that happen to good people.

How can I miss you if you won't go away?

Sorry if I looked interested. I'm not.

If we are what we eat, I'm fast, cheap and easy.

Subject: Actual Headlines

1) Include Your Children When Baking Cookies

2) Police Begin Campaign to Run Down Jaywalkers

3) Safety Experts Say School Bus Passengers Should Be Belted

4) Iraqi Head Seeks Arms

5) Teacher Strikes Idle Kids

6) Enraged Cow Injures Farmer With Ax

7) Plane Too Close to Ground, Crash Probe Told

8) Miners Refuse to Work After Death

9) Juvenile Court to Try Shooting Defendant

10) Two Sisters Reunited After 18 Years in Checkout Counter

11) Killer Sentenced to Die for Second Time in 10 Years

12) If Strike Isn't Settled Quickly, It May Last a While

13) Couple Slain; Police Suspect Homicide

14) Red Tape Holds Up New Bridges

15) Typhoon Rips Through Cemetery; Hundreds Dead

16) Astronaut Takes Blame for Gas in Spacecraft

17) Ban On Soliciting Dead in Trotwood

18) Local High School Dropouts Cut in Half

19) New Vaccine May Contain Rabies

20) Hospitals are Sued by 7 Foot Doctors

Read This; It's Funny!!

Subject: T-Shirt Slogans

1. "Frankly, Scallop, I Don't Give a Clam." (Seen on Cape Cod)

2. "That's It! I'm Calling Grandma!" (Seen on an 8 year old)

3. "Wrinkled Was Not One of the Things I Wanted to Be When I Grew Up"

4. "Procrastinate Now."

5. "Rehab Is for Quitters."

6. "My Dog Can Lick Anyone."

7. "I Have a Degree in Liberal Arts - Do You Want Fries With That?"

8. "Party - My Crib - Two A.M." (On a baby-size shirt)

9. "Finally 21, and Legally Able to Do Everything I've Been Doing Since 15."

10. "ALL MEN ARE IDIOTS, AND I MARRIED THEIR KING."

11. "FAILURE IS NOT AN OPTION. It comes bundled with the software."

12. "I'M OUT OF ESTROGEN AND I'VE GOT A GUN."

13. "A hangover is the wrath of grapes."

14. "A journey of a thousand miles begins with a cash advance."

15. "STUPIDITY IS NOT A HANDICAP. Park elsewhere!"

16. "Quoting one is plagiarism. Quoting many is research."

17. "They call it 'PMS' because 'Mad Cow Disease' was already taken."

18. "He who dies with the most toys is nonetheless dead."

19. "Time's fun when you're having flies...Kermit the Frog."

20. "FOR SALE: Iraqi rifle. Never fired. Dropped once."

21. "HECK IS WHERE PEOPLE GO WHO DON'T BELIEVE IN GOSH."

22. "A PICTURE IS WORTH A THOUSAND WORDS, but it uses up a thousand times the memory."

23. "The Meek shall inherit the earth.... after we're through with it."

24. "Time flies like an arrow. Fruit flies like a banana."

25. "HAM AND EGGS - A day's work for a chicken; A lifetime commitment for a pig."

26. "The trouble with life is there's no background music."

27. "IF THERE IS NO GOD, WHO POPS UP THE NEXT KLEENEX?"

28. "Suicidal Twin Kills Sister By Mistake!"

29. "The original point-and-click interface was a Smith Wesson."

30. "MY WILD OATS HAVE TURNED TO SHREDDED WHEAT."

31. "Computer programmers don't byte, they nibble a bit."

32. "MOP AND GLOW - Floor wax used by Three-Mile-Island cleanup team."

33. "Nyquil - The stuffy, sneezy, why-the-heck-is-the-room-spinning medicine."

34. "My husband and I divorced over religious differences.
    He thought he was God, and I didn't."

Subject: Rejected Hallmark Cards

"How could two people as beautiful you have such an ugly baby?"

"I've always wanted to have someone to hold, someone to love. After having met you, I've changed my mind."

"I must admit, you brought Religion in my life. I never believed in Hell until I met you."

"As the days go by, I think of how lucky I am that you're not here to ruin it for me."

"Thanks for being a part of my life!!! I never knew what evil was before this!"

"Congratulations on your promotion. Before you go, would you like to take this knife out of my back? You'll probably need it again."

"Someday I hope to get married, but not to you."

"Happy Birthday! You look great for your age... Almost Lifelike!

"When we were together, you always said you'd die for me. Now that we've broke up, I think it's time you kept your promise."

"We have been friends for a very long time; what say we call it quits?"

"I'm so miserable without you, it's almost like you're here."

"You are such a good friend that if we were on a sinking ship and there was only one life jacket.... I'd miss you heaps and think of you often."

"If you didn't have any money, I'd still love you. And miss you very much."

Answer This

Subject: Brain Exercise..77
Subject: Jedi Mind Trick...79
Subject: Quick Eye Exam 81

Subject: Brain Exercise

Exercise of the brain is as important as exercise of the muscles.

As we grow older, it's important that we keep mentally alert. The saying; "If you don't use it, you will lose it" also applies to the brain, so.........

Below is a very private way to gage your loss or non-loss of intelligence.

So take the following test presented here and determine if you are losing it or are still a MENSA candidate.

OK, relax, clear your mind and....... begin.

1. What do you put in a toaster?
The answer is bread. If you said "toast", then give up now and go do something else. Try not to hurt yourself. If you said, "bread", go to question 2.

2. Say "silk" five times. Now spell "silk". What do cows drink?
Answer: Cows drink water. If you said "milk", please do not attempt the next question. Your brain is obviously overstressed and may even overheat. It may be that you need to content yourself with reading something more appropriate such as "Children's World." If you said, "water" then proceed to question three.

3. If a red house is made from red bricks and a blue house is made from blue bricks and a pink house is made from pink bricks and a black house is made from black bricks, what is a greenhouse made from?
Answer: Greenhouses are made from glass. If you said "green bricks", what the devil are you still doing here reading these questions????? ..If you said "glass", then go on to question four.

4. Twenty years ago, a plane is flying at 20,000 feet over Germany. If you will recall, Germany at the time was politically divided into West Germany and East Germany. Anyway, during the flight, TWO of the engines fail. The pilot, realizing that the last remaining engine is also failing, decides on a crash landing procedure. Unfortunately the engine fails before he has time and the plane crashes smack in the middle of "no man's land" between East Germany and West Germany. Where would you

Read This; It's Funny!!

bury the survivors - East Germany or West Germany or in "no man's land"?

Answer: You don't, of course, bury survivors. If you said ANYTHING else, you are a real dunce and you must NEVER try to rescue anyone from a plane crash. Your efforts would not be appreciated. If you said, "Don't bury the survivors" then proceed to the next question.

5. If the hour hand on a clock moves 1/60th of a degree every minute then how many degrees will the hour hand move in one hour?

Answer: One degree. If you said "360 degrees" or anything other than "one degree", you are to be congratulated on getting this far, but you are obviously out of your league. Turn your pencil in and exit the room. Everyone else proceed to the final question.

6. Without using a calculator - You are driving a bus from London to Milford Haven in Wales. In London, 17 people get on the bus. In Reading, six people get off the bus and nine people get on. In Swindon, two people get off and four get on. In Cardiff, 11 people get off and 16 people get on. In Swansea, three people get off and five people get on. In Carmathen, six people get off and three get on. You then arrive at Milford Haven. What was the name of the bus driver?

Answer: Oh for goodness sake! It was you, you dummy. Read the first line!!!

78

Subject: Jedi Mind Trick

This little Jedi mind trick is kinda freaky, till you think about it a little while. Then it's even more weird. Just follow the instructions below:

DON'T scroll down too fast-do it slowly and follow the instructions below exactly, do the math in your head as fast as you can. It may help to say the answers aloud quietly.

FOLLOW these instructions one at a time and as QUICKLY as you can!

What is:

2+2?

4+4?

8+8?

16+16?

Quick! Pick a number between 12 and 5

Got it?

Now scroll down...

The number you picked was 7, right?
Isn't that weird???
Free will or synaptic wiring? You be the judge. Check out the following exercise, guaranteed to freak you out. There's no trick or surprise. Just follow these instructions, and answer the questions one at a time and as quickly as you can! Again, as quickly as you can but don't advance until you've done each of them...really.
Now, ARROW down (but not too fast, you might miss something)...

What is:

1+5

Read This; It's Funny!!

2+4

3+3

4+2

5+1

Now repeat saying the number 6 to yourself as fast as you can for 15 seconds. Then scroll down.

QUICK!!! THINK OF A VEGETABLE! Then arrow down.

Keep going.

You're thinking of a carrot right? If not, you're among the 2% of the population whose minds are warped enough to think of something else. 98% of people will answer with carrot when given this exercise. Freaky, huh?

Subject: Quick Eye Exam

This will blow your mind...!

Just do it - don't cheat !!!!!!!!!!!!

Try this its actually quite good   But don't cheat !

Count the number of 'F's in the following text:

FINISHED FILES ARE THE RESULT OF YEARS OF SCIENTIFIC STUDY COMBINED WITH THE EXPERIENCE OF YEARS

Managed it?

.... Scroll down only after you have counted them!

OK?

How many?

Three?

Wrong, there are SIX - no joke!

Read again

FINISHED FILES ARE THE RESULT OF YEARS OF SCIENTIFIC STUDY COMBINED WITH THE EXPERIENCE OF YEARS

The reasoning is further down...

The brain cannot process the word "OF".

Incredible or what?

Anyone who counts all six 'F' on the first go is a genius, Three is normal.

Glorified Calculators

Subject: Computer Gender 83
Subject: Computer Haiku 84
Subject: Dr. Seuss Tech 86
Subject: LAZY Virus 87
Subject: Remember When 88
Subject: Spell Checker 89
Subject: Who's on Start? 90
Subject: Windows Southern Edition 92

Subject: Computer Gender

An English teacher was explaining to his students the concept of gender association in the English language. He stated that hurricanes at one time were all given feminine names and that ships and planes are usually referred to as "she."

One of the students raised his hand and asked, "What gender is a computer?" Not having a ready answer, the teacher divided the class into two groups, males in one and females in the other, and asked each group to decide whether a computer should be considered masculine or feminine. Both groups were asked to give four reasons for their recommendation.

The group of women concluded that computers should be considered masculine because:

1. In order to get their attention, you have to turn them on.
2. They have a lot of data but are still clueless.
3. They are supposed to help you solve your problems, but half the time they ARE the problem.
4. As soon as you commit to one, you realize that, if you had waited a little longer, you could have had a better model.

The men, on the other hand, decided that computers should be considered feminine because:

1. No one but their creator understands their internal logic.
2. The native language they use to communicate with other computers is incomprehensible to everyone else.
3. Even your smallest mistakes are stored in long-term memory for later retrieval.
4. As soon as you make a commitment to one, you find yourself spending half your paycheck on accessories for it.

Read This; It's Funny!!

Subject: Computer Haiku

In Japan, Sony Vaio machines have replaced the impersonal and unhelpful Microsoft error messages with their own Japanese haiku poetry, each only 17 syllables.

A file that big?
It might be very useful.
But now it is all gone.

The Web site you seek
Cannot be located but
Countless more exist.

Chaos reigns within.
Reflect, repent, and reboot.
Order shall return.

ABORTED effort:
Close all that you have worked on.
You ask way too much.

Windows 98 crashed.
I 'm the Blue Screen of Death.
No one hears your screams.

Yesterday it worked.
Today it is not working.
Windows is like that.

First snow, then silence.
This thousand dollar screen dies
So beautifully.

With searching comes loss
And the presence of absence:
"My Novel" not found.

The Tao that is seen
Is not the true Tao, until
You bring fresh toner.

Stay the patient course.
Of little worth is your ire.
The network is down.

A crash reduces
Your expensive computer
To a simple stone.

Three things are certain:
Death, taxes, and lost data.
Guess which has occurred.

You step in the stream,
But the water has moved on.
This page is not here.

Out of memory.
We wish to hold the whole sky,
But we never will.

Having been erased,
The document you're seeking
Must now be retyped.

Serious error.
Serious error.
All shortcuts have disappeared.

Read This; It's Funny!!

Subject: Dr. Seuss Tech

What if Dr. Seuss did technical writing?
(You really have to read this one out loud to appreciate it)

If a packet hits a pocket on a socket on a port,
and the bus is interrupted as a very last resort,
and the address of the memory makes your floppy disk abort,
then the socket packet pocket has an error to report.

If your cursor finds a menu item followed by a dash,
and the double-clicking icon puts your window in the trash,
and your data is corrupted 'cause the index doesn't hash,
then your situation's hopeless and your system's gonna crash!

If the label on the cable on the table at your house,
says the network is connected to the button on your mouse,
but your packets want to tunnel on another protocol,
that's repeatedly rejected by the printer down the hall,
and your screen is all distorted by the side effects of gauss,
so your icons in the window are as wavy as a souse,
then you may as well reboot and go out with a bang,
'cause as sure as I'm a poet, the sucker's gonna hang!

When the copy of your floppy's getting sloppy on the disk,
and the microcode instructions cause unnecessary risk,
then you have to flash your memory and you'll want to RAM
your ROM.
Quickly turn off the computer and be sure to tell your mom!

Subject: LAZY Virus

You have just received the "LAZY Virus"!!!

As we don't have any programming experience, this virus works on the honor system.

Please delete all the files on your hard drive, then manually forward this virus to everyone on your mailing list.

Thanks for your cooperation.

Read This; It's Funny!!

Subject: Remember When

A computer was something on TV
from a science fiction show of note
a window was something you hated to clean...
And ram was the cousin of a goat....

Meg was the name of my girlfriend
and gig was a job for the nights
now they all mean different things
and that really mega bytes

An application was for employment
a program was a TV show
a cursor used profanity
a keyboard was a piano

Memory was something that you lost with age
a cd was a bank account
and if you had a 3 1/2" floppy
you hoped nobody found out

Compress was something you did to the garbage
not something you did to a file
and if you unzipped anything in public
you'd be in jail for a while

Log on was adding wood to the fire
hard drive was a long trip on the road
a mouse pad was where a mouse lived
and a backup happened to your commode

Cut you did with a pocket knife
paste you did with glue
a web was a spider's home
and a virus was the flu

I guess I'll stick to my pad and paper
and the memory in my head
I hear nobody's been killed in a computer crash
but when it happens they wish they were dead

Subject: Spell Checker

Eye halve a spelling chequer
It came with my pea sea
It plainly marques four my revue
Miss steaks eye kin knot sea.

Eye strike a key and type a word
And weight four it two say
Weather eye am wrong oar write
It shows me strait a weigh.

As soon as a mist ache is maid
It nose bee fore two long
And eye can put the error rite
Its rarely ever wrong.

Eye have run this poem threw it
I am shore your pleased two no
Its letter perfect in it's weigh
My chequer tolled me sew.

Read This; It's Funny!!

Subject: Who's on Start?

Costello: Hey, Abbott!
Abbott: Yes, Lou?

Costello: I just got my first computer.
Abbott: That's great, Lou. What did you get?

Costello: A 2.6 gigahertz P-4, with 1 Gig of DDR-RAM, 128 Meg
video, 100 Gig hard drive, a 52X CD-BURNER and a DVD.
Abbott: That's terrific, Lou.

Costello: But I don't know what any of it means!
Abbott: You will in time.

Costello: That's exactly why I'm here to see you.
Abbott: Oh?

Costello: I heard that you're a real computer expert.
Abbott: Well, I don't know . . .

Costello: Yes-sir-ee. You know your stuff. And you're going to
train me.
Abbott: Really?

Costello: Uh huh. And I am here for my first lesson.
Abbott: O.K. Lou. What do you want to know?

Costello: I am having no problem turning it on, but I heard that
you should be very careful how you turn it off.
Abbott: That's true.

Costello: So, here I am working on my new computer and I
want to turn it off. What do I do?
Abbott: Well, first you press the Start button, and then . . .

Costello: No, I told you I want to turn it off.
Abbott: I know, you press the Start button . . .

Costello: Wait a second. I want to turn it Off. I know how to
start it. So tell me what to do.
Abbott: I did.

90

Costello: When?
Abbott: When I told you to press the Start button.

Costello: Why should I press the Start button?
Abbott: To shut off the computer.

Costello: I press Start to stop?
Abbott: Well, Start doesn't actually stop the computer.

Costello: I knew it! So what do I press?
Abbott: Start.

Costello: Start what?
Abbott: Start button.

Costello: Start button to do what?
Abbott: Shut down.

Costello: You don't have to get rude!
Abbott: No, no, no! That's not what I meant.

Costello: Then say what you mean.
Abbott: To shut down the computer, press . . .

Costello: Don't say, "Start!"
Abbott: Then what do you want me to say?

Costello: Look, if I want to turn off the computer, I am willing to press the Stop button, the End button and Cease and Desist button, but no one in their right mind presses Start to Stop.
Abbott: But that's what you do.

Costello: And you probably Go at Stop signs, and Stop at green lights.
Abbott: Don't be ridiculous.

Costello: I'm being ridiculous? Well, I think it's about time we started this conversation.
Abbott: What are you talking about?

Costello: I am starting this conversation right now. Good-bye.

Read This; It's Funny!!

Subject: Windows Southern Edition

Dear Consumers:

It has come to our attention that a few copies of the WINDOWS SOUTHERN EDITION may have accidentally been shipped outside the South. If you have one of these, you may need some help understanding the commands.

The southern edition may be recognized by the unique opening screen. It reads "WINDERS," with a background picture of General Robert E. Lee superimposed on a Confederate flag. It is shipped with a Dukes of Hazzard screen saver. Also note:

The Recycle Bin is labeled "Outhouse."
* My Computer is called "This Dumb Contraption"
* Dial up Networking is called "Good Ol' Boys"
* Control Panel is known as the "The Dashboard"
* Hard Drive is referred to as "4 Wheel Drive"
* Floppies are "them little ol plastic disc thangs"
* Instead of an error message a "garbage bag and a roll of duct tape" pops up.

CHANGES IN TERMINOLOGY IN SOUTHERN EDITION:
* OK: ats aw-right
* Cancel: stopdat
* Reset: try 'er agin
* Yes: yep
* No: nope
* Find: hunt fer it
* Get: fetch it
* Go to: over yonder
* Back: back yonder
* Help: hep me outa here!
* Stop: kwitit
* Start: crank 'er up!
* Settings: sittins
* Programs: stuff dat duz stuff
* Documents: stuff ah done did

Also note that SOUTHERN EDITION does not recognize capital letters or punctuation marks. Some programs that are exclusive to Winders :

* tiperiter: A word processing program
* colerin book: a graphics program
* cyferin mersheen: calculator
* outhouse paper: notepad
* jupe-box: CD Player
* iner-net: Microsoft Explorer
* pichers: A graphics viewer
* irs: MS accounting software
* irs2: MS accounting software with hidden files
* tax records: usually an empty file
* coon dog: American kennel club records

You'll recognize WINDERS SOUTHERN EDITION, as it comes pre-loaded with certain "Favorites" for browsing the World Wide Web.

* Fishin': Bass Anglers Sportsman Society
* NRA: National Rifle Association
* Shotgun: Remington Arms home page
* Riffel: Winchester home page
* Pistul: Smith & Wesson home page
* Truck: Ford & Chevy dealers by zip code
* House: Mobile home repair services & movers by zip code
* Cuzzins: Complete database of southern residents (extremely long download time)
* Racin': NASCAR schedule with 20 TV stations that carry the races
* Car 'n truck parts: Junk yards by zip code
* Doc: Veterinarians by zip code

We regret any inconvenience it may have caused if you received a copy of WINDERS SOUTHERN EDITION. You may return it to Microsoft for a replacement. I hope this helps all y'all!

Billy Bob Gates

Our Jokes, Ourselves

Subject: Blond Revenge 95
Subject: Jail 96
Subject: Hero 97
Subject: Rod and Reel 98
Subject: Special Pig 99
Subject: Pillsbury Doughboy 100
Subject: Right Age for Cussing 101
Subject: How to Handle Stress 102

Subject: Blond Revenge

What's black and blue and brown and laying in a ditch?
  A brunette who's told too many blonde jokes.

What do you call going on a blind date with a brunette?
  Brown-bagging it.

What's the real reason a brunette keeps her figure?
  No one else wants it.

Why are so many blonde jokes one-liners ?
  So brunettes can remember them.

What do you call a brunette in a room full of blondes?
  Invisible.

What's a brunette's mating call?
  "Has the blonde left yet? "

Why didn't Indians scalp brunettes?
  The hair from a buffalo's butt was more manageable.

Why is the brunette considered an evil color?
  When was the last time you saw a blonde witch?

What do brunettes miss most about a great party?
  The invitation.

What do you call a good looking man with a brunette?
  A hostage.

Who makes bras for brunettes?
  Fisher-Price.

Why are brunettes so proud of their hair?
  It matches their mustache.

Read This; It's Funny!!

Subject: Jail

Three convicts were on the way to prison. They were each allowed to take one item with them to help them occupy their time whilst stuck behind bars. On the bus, one turned to another and said, "So, what did you bring?"

The second convict pulled out a box of paints and stated that he intended to paint anything he could. He wanted to become the "Grandma Moses of Jail."

Then he asked the first, "What did you bring?"

The first convict pulled out a deck of cards and grinned and said, "I brought cards. I can play poker, solitaire and gin, and any number of games."

The third convict was sitting quietly aside grinning to himself. The other two took notice and asked, "Why are you so smug? What did you bring?"

The guy pulled out a box of tampons and smiled. "I brought these."

The other two were puzzled and asked, "What can you do with those?"

He grinned and pointed to the box and said, "Well according to the box, I can go horseback riding, swimming, roller-skating..."

Subject: Hero

Two boys are playing football in Denver City Park when one is attacked by a rabid Rottweiler. Thinking quickly, the other boy rips a board off a nearby fence, wedges it down the dog's collar and twists, breaking the dog's neck.

A reporter, who was strolling by, sees the incident, and rushes over to interview the boy. "Young Broncos Fan Saves Friend From Vicious Animal," he starts writing in his notebook.

"But I'm not a Broncos fan," the little hero replied.

"Sorry, since we are in Denver I just assumed you were." said the reporter. He erases the first headline and tries again. "Little Rockies Fan Rescues Friend From Horrific Attack" he writes in his notebook.

"But I'm not a Rockies fan either," the boy said.

"I assumed everyone in Denver was either for the Broncos or Rockies. What team do you root for?" the reporter asked.

"I'm a Cowboys fan." the child said.

The reporter starts a new sheet in his notebook and writes, "Little Redneck Bastard Kills Beloved Family Pet."

Read This; It's Funny!!

Subject: Rod and Reel

A woman goes into Wal-Mart to buy a rod and reel. She doesn't know which one to get so she just grabs one and goes over to the register. There is a Wal-Mart "associate" standing there with dark shades on.

She says, "Excuse me sir...can you tell me anything about this rod and reel?"

He says, "Ma'am I'm blind but if you will drop it on the counter I can tell you everything you need to know about it from the sound that it makes."

She didn't believe him, but dropped it on the counter anyway. He said, "That's a 6' graphite rod with a Zebco 202 reel and 10 lb. test line... It's a good all around rod and reel and it's $20.00".

She says, "That's amazing that you can tell all that just by the sound of it dropping on the counter. I think it's what I'm looking for so I'll take it."

He walks behind the counter to the register, and in the meantime the woman farts.

At first, she is embarrassed but then realizes that there is no way he could tell it was her...being blind he wouldn't know that she was the only person around.

He rings up the sale and says, "That will be $25.50."

She says, "But didn't you say it was $20.00?"

He says, "Yes ma'am, the rod and reel is $20.00, the duck call is $3.00, and the catfish stink bait is $2.50."

Subject: Special Pig

Farmer Jones got out of his car and while heading for his friend's door, noticed a pig with a wooden leg. His curiosity roused, he ask, "Fred, how'd that pig get a wooden leg?"

"Well Michael, that's a mighty special pig! A while back a wild boar attacked me while I was walking in the woods. That pig there came a runnin', went after that boar and chased him away. Saved my life!"

"And the boar tore up his leg?"

"No he was fine after that. But a bit later we had that fire. Started in the shed up against the barn. Well, that ole pig started squealin' like he was stuck, woke us up, and 'fore we got out here, the darn thing had herded the other animals out of the barn and saved 'em all!"

"So that's when he hurt his leg, huh, Fred?"

"No, Michael. He was a might winded, though. When my tractor hit a rock and rolled down the hill into the pond I was knocked clean out. When I came to, that pig had dove into the pond and dragged me out 'fore I drowned. Sure did save my life."

"And that was when he hurt his leg?"

"Oh no, he was fine. Cleaned him up, too."

"OK, Fred. So just tell me. How did he get the wooden leg?"

"Well", the farmer tells him, "A pig like that, you don't want to eat all at once."

Read This; It's Funny!!

Subject: Pillsbury Doughboy

Such a sad note...

It is with a heavy heart that I pass on the following.

The Pillsbury Doughboy died yesterday of a yeast infection and complications from repeated pokes in the belly. He was 71.

Doughboy was buried in a lightly greased coffin. Dozens of celebrities turned out to pay their respects, including Mrs. Butterworth, Hungry Jack, the California Raisins, Betty Crocker, the Hostess Twinkies, and Captain Crunch.

The gravesite was piled high with flours.

His long-time friend, Aunt Jemima, delivered the eulogy, describing Doughboy as a man who never knew how much he was kneaded.

Doughboy rose quickly in show business, but his later life was filled with turnovers. He was not considered a very "smart" cookie, wasting much of his dough on half-baked schemes.

Despite being a little flaky at times, he even still, as a crusty old man, was considered a roll model for millions.

Toward the end it was thought he would rise again, but alas, it was not to be.

Doughboy is survived by his wife, Play Dough; two children, John Dough and Jane Dough; plus they had one in the oven.

He is also survived by his elderly father, Pop Tart.

The funeral was held at about 3:50 for twenty minutes.

Subject: Right Age for Cussing

A 6-year-old and a 4-year-old are upstairs in their bedroom.

"You know what?" says the 6-year-old. "I think it's about time we start cussing."

The 4-year-old nods his head in approval.

The 6-year-old continues. "When we go downstairs for breakfast I'm going to say "hell" and you say "ass."

"OK!" The 4 year old agrees with enthusiasm.

Their mother walks into the kitchen and asks the 6-year-old what he wants for breakfast.

"Aw hell, Mom, I guess I'll have some Cheerios."

WHACK! He flies out of his chair, tumbles across the kitchen floor, gets up, and runs upstairs crying his eyes out, with his mother in hot pursuit, slapping his rear every step. The mom locks him in his room and shouts "You can just stay there till I let you out!"

She then comes back downstairs, looks at the 4-year-old, and asks with a stern voice, "And what do YOU want for breakfast, young man?

"I don't know," he blubbers, "But you can bet your fat ass it won't be Cheerios."

Read This; It's Funny!!

Subject: How to Handle Stress

A Visualization

Picture yourself near a stream.

Birds are softly chirping in the crisp, cool mountain air.

Nothing can bother you here.
No one knows this secret place.
You are in total seclusion from that place called "the world."
The soothing sound of a gentle waterfall fills the air with a cascade of serenity.

The water is clear.
You can easily make out the face of the person whose head you're holding under the water.
There now......feeling better?

How Things Get Done

Subject: How to Annoy People 104
Subject: How to Screw Up an Interview 106
Subject: How To Keep A Healthy Level Of Insanity 108
Subject: 10 Ways To Terrify A Telemarketer 109

Read This; It's Funny!!

Subject: How to Annoy People

29 Ways to Annoy People (For those who don't know how.)

1.   Leave the copy machine set to reduce 200%, extra dark, 7 inch paper, 99 copies.
2. If you have a glass eye, tap on it with your pen while talking to others.
3.   Sing along at the Opera.
4. Insist on keeping your car windshield wipers running in all weather conditions "to keep them tuned up".
5.   Reply to everything someone says with "that's what YOU think".
6.   Practice making fax and modem noises.
7.   Highlight irrelevant material in scientific papers and cc. them to your boss.
8. Make beeping noises when a large person backs up.
9. Signal that a conversation is over by clamping your hands over your ears.
10. Disassemble your pen and "accidentally" flip the cartridge across the room.
11. Holler random numbers while someone is counting.
12. Adjust the tint on your TV so that all the people are green, and insist to others that you "like it that way".
13. Staple papers in the middle of the page.
14. Publicly investigate just how slowly you can make a croaking noise.
15. Honk and wave to strangers.
16 Decline to be seated at a restaurant, and simply eat their complimentary mints by the cash register.
17. TYPE ONLY IN UPPERCASE.
18. type only in lower case.
19. Buy a large number of orange traffic cones and reroute whole streets.
20. Repeat the following conversation a dozen times: "Do you hear that?", "What?", "Never mind, it's gone now".
21. As much as possible, skip rather than walk.
22. Try playing the William Tell Overture by tapping on the bottom of your chin. When nearly done, announce, "No, wait, I messed it up" and repeat.
23. While making presentations, occasionally bob your head like a parakeet.

24. In the memo field of all your checks, write "for sensual massage".

25. Stomp on little plastic ketchup packets.

26. Go to a poetry recital and ask why each poem doesn't rhyme.

27. Ask your co-workers mysterious questions and then scribble the answers in a notebook. Mutter something about "psychological profiles".

28. Tell your friends 4 days prior, that you can't attend their party because you're not in the mood.

Read This; It's Funny!!

Subject: How to Screw Up an Interview

We've all been interviewed for jobs. And, we've all spent most of those interviews thinking about what not to do. Don't bite your nails. Don't fidget. Don't interrupt. Don't belch.

If we did any of the don'ts, we knew we'd disqualify ourselves instantly. But some job applicants go light years beyond this.

We surveyed top personnel executives of 100 major American corporations and asked for stories of unusual behavior by job applicants.

The lowlights:

1. "... stretched out on the floor to fill out the job application."

2. "She wore a Walkman and said she could listen to me and the music at the same time."

3. " A balding candidate abruptly excused himself. Returned to office a few minutes later, wearing a hairpiece."

4. "... asked to see interviewer's resume to see if the personnel executive was qualified to judge the candidate."

5. "... announced she hadn't had lunch and proceeded to eat a hamburger and French fries in the interviewer's office - wiping the ketchup on her sleeve"

6. "Stated that, if he were hired, he would demonstrate his loyalty by having the corporate logo tattooed on his forearm."

7. "Interrupted to phone his therapist for advice on answering specific interview questions."

8. "When I asked him about his hobbies, he stood up and started tap dancing around my office."

9. "At the end of the interview, while I stood there dumbstruck, he went through my purse, took out a brush, brushed his hair, and left."

106

10. "... pulled out a Polaroid camera and snapped a flash picture of me. Said he collected photos of everyone who interviewed him."

11. "Said he wasn't interested because the position paid too much."

12. "While I was on a long-distance phone call, the applicant took out a copy of Penthouse, and looked through the photos only, stopping longest at the centerfold."

13. "During the interview, an alarm clock went off from the candidate's brief case. He took it out, shut it off, apologized and said he had to leave for another interview."

14. "A telephone call came in for the job applicant. It was from his wife. His side of the conversation went like this: "Which company? When do I start? What's the salary?" I said, "I assume you're not interested in conducting the interview any further." He promptly responded, "I am as long as you'll pay me more. "I didn't hire him, but later found out there was no other job offer. It was a scam to get a higher offer."

15. "His attaché [case] opened when he picked it up and the contents spilled, revealing ladies' undergarments and assorted makeup and perfume."

16. "Candidate said he really didn't want to get a job, but the unemployment office needed proof that he was looking for one."

17. "... asked who the lovely babe was, pointing to the picture on my desk. When I said it was my wife, he asked if she was home now and wanted my phone number. I called security,"

18. "Pointing to a black case he carried into my office, he said that if he was not hired, the bomb would go off. Disbelieving, I began to state why he would never be hired and that I was going to call the police. He then reached down to the case, flipped a switch and ran. No one was injured, but I did need to get a new desk."

I don't mind going nowhere as long as it's an interesting path.

Read This; It's Funny!!

Subject: How To Keep A Healthy Level Of Insanity

1. At lunch time, sit in your parked car with sunglasses on and point a hair dryer at passing cars. See if they slow down.
2. Page yourself over the intercom. Don't disguise your voice.
3. Every time someone asks you to do something, ask if they want fries with that.
4. Put your garbage can on your desk and label it "in"
5. Put decaf in the coffee maker for 3 weeks. Once everyone has gotten over their caffeine addictions, switch to espresso.
6. Finish all your sentences with "in accordance with the prophecy."
7. dont use any punctuation marks
8. As often as possible, skip rather than walk.
9. Ask people what sex they are. Laugh hysterically after they answer.
10. Specify that your drive-through order is "to go".
11. Sing along at the opera.
12. Go to a poetry recital and ask why the poems don't rhyme.
13. Put mosquito netting around your work area. Play a tape of jungle sounds all day.
14. Have your coworkers address you by your wrestling name, Rock Hard Kim.
15. When the money comes out the ATM, scream I won!", "I won!" "3rd time this week!!!!!"
16. When leaving the zoo, start running towards the parking lot, yelling "run for your lives, they're loose!!"
17. Tell your children over dinner, "Due to the economy, we are going to have to let one of you go."
And the final way to keep a healthy level of insanity...
18. Send this e-mail to everyone in your address book, even if they sent it to you or asked you not to send them stuff like this.

Subject: 10 Ways To Terrify A Telemarketer

10. When they ask "How are you today?" Tell them! "I'm so glad you asked because no one these days seems to care, and I have all these problems; my arthritis is acting up, my eyelashes are sore, my dog just died..."

9. If they say they're John Doe from XYZ Company, ask them to spell their name. Then ask them to spell the company name. Then ask them where it is located. Continue asking them personal questions or questions about their company for as long as necessary.

8. Cry out in surprise, "Judy! Is that you? Oh my God! Judy, how have you been?" Hopefully, this will give Judy a few brief moments of pause as she tries to figure out where the h-l she could know you from.

7. If MCI calls trying to get you to sign up for the Family and Friends Plan, reply, in a SINISTER voice , "I don't have any friends ..would you be my friend?"

6. If they want to loan you money, tell them you just filed for bankruptcy and you could sure use some money.

5. Tell the telemarketer you are on "home incarceration" and ask if they could bring you a case of beer and some chips. (LOVE THIS ONE!)

4. After the telemarketer gives their spiel, ask him/her to marry you. When they get all flustered, tell them that you could not just give our credit card number to a complete stranger.

3. Tell the telemarketer you are busy at the moment and ask them if they will give you their HOME phone number so you can call them back. When the telemarketer explains that they cannot give out their HOME number, you say "I guess you don't want anyone bothering you at home, right?" The telemarketer will agree and you say, "Now you know how I feel!" Say good bye and hang up.

2. Insist that the caller is really your buddy Leon, playing a joke. "Come on Leon, cut it out! Seriously, Leon, how's your momma?"

And first and foremost:

1. Tell them to talk VERY SLOWLY, because you want to write EVERY WORD down.

Information You Can Use

Subject: Anagrams 111
Subject: Broker's Tips 112
Subject: Cat Wisdom 113
Subject: Chocolate is a Vegetable 114
Subject: Daffynitions.. 115
Subject: More Daffynitions 116
Subject: New Dog Cross Breeds 118
Subject: Gender 120
Subject: Questions for the Wise... 122
Subject: Rules for Writers.. 123
Subject: Today's Stock Market Report 125
Subject: Weather by Degree 126
Subject: The Y1K Crisis 128

Subject: Anagrams

This is really spooky.....

An anagram, as you all know, is a word or phrase made by rearranging the letters of another word or phrase.

The following are exceptionally clever. Someone out there either has way too much time to waste or is deadly at Scrabble.

Word -	When you rearrange the letters
Dormitory	Dirty Room
Desperation	A Rope Ends It
The Morse Code	Here come Dots
Slot Machines	Cash Lost in 'em
Animosity	Is No Amity
Mother-in-law	Woman Hitler
Snooze Alarms	Alas! No More Z's
Alec Guinness	Genuine Class
Semolina	Is No Meal
The Public Art Galleries	Large Picture Halls, I bet
A Decimal Point	I'm a Dot in Place
The Earthquakes	That Queer Shake
Eleven plus two	Twelve plus one
Contradiction	Accord not in it
Astronomer	Moon Starer
Princess Diana	End Is A Car Spin

AND HERE IS THE MOST INTRIGUING PART

Year Two Thousand	A Year To Shut Down

Read This; It's Funny!!

Subject: Broker's Tips

I just received this from my broker. I normally don't pass stock tips on, but I thought this exception would be ok. If you hold any of the following stock, you may want to review.

American Can Co.

Interstate Water Co.

National Gas Co.

Northern Tissue Co.

Due to the uncertain market conditions, at this present time, we advise you to sit tight on your American Can, hold your water, and let go of your gas.

You may be interested to know that Northern Tissue touched a new bottom today, and millions were wiped clean.

Subject: Cat Wisdom

CAT WISDOM

_____

1. Cats do what they want, when they want.
2. They rarely listen to you.
3. They're totally unpredictable.
4. They whine when they are not happy.
5. When you want to play, they want to be alone.
6. When you want to be alone, they want to play.
7. They expect you to cater to their every whim.
8. They're moody.
9. They leave hair everywhere.
10. They drive you nuts.

Conclusion: They're like little, tiny women in cheap fur coats.

Read This; It's Funny!!

Subject: Chocolate is a Vegetable

Chocolate is derived from cocoa beans.

Bean = vegetable.

Sugar is derived from either sugar cane or sugar BEETS.

Both of them are plants, in the vegetable category.

Thus, chocolate is a vegetable.

To go one step further, chocolate candy bars also contain milk, which is dairy. So candy bars are a health food.

Chocolate-covered raisins, cherries, orange slices and strawberries all count as fruit, so eat as many as you want.

Remember: "STRESSED" spelled backward is "DESSERTS"

Send this to four women and you will lose 2 pounds.
Send this to all the women you know (or ever knew), and you will lose 10 pounds.

(If you delete this message, you will gain 10 pounds immediately.)

"That's why I had to pass this on - - - - - I didn't want to risk it."

Subject: Daffynitions

The Washington Post's "Style Invitational" asked readers to take any word from the dictionary, alter it by adding, subtracting or changing one letter, and supply a new definition.

Here are some recent winners:

Reintarnation: Coming back to life as a hillbilly.

Giraffiti: Vandalism spray-painted very, very high. . . .

Tatyr: A lecherous Mr. Potato Head.

Sarchasm: The gulf between the author of sarcastic wit and the recipient who doesn't get it.

Inoculatte: To take coffee intravenously when you are running late.

Hipatitis: Terminal coolness.

Osteopornosis: A degenerate disease.

Burglesque: A poorly planned break-in. (See: Watergate)

Karmageddon: It's like, when everybody is sending off all these really bad vibes, right? And then, like, the Earth explodes and it's like a serious bummer.

Glibido: All talk and no action.

Dopeler effect: The tendency of stupid ideas to seem smarter when they come at you rapidly.

Intaxication: Euphoria at getting a refund from the IRS, which lasts until you realize it was your money to start with.

Read This; It's Funny!!

Subject: More Daffynitions

1. AQUADEXTROUS (ak wa deks' trus) adj. Possessing the ability to turn the bathroom faucet on and off with your toes.

2. CARPERPITULATION (kar' pur pet u a shun) n. The act, when vacuuming, of running over a string or a piece of lint at least a dozen times, reaching over and picking it up, examining it, then putting it back down to give the vacuum one more chance.

3. DISCONFECT (dis kon fekt') v. To sterilize the piece of candy you dropped on the floor by blowing on it, assuming this will somehow 'remove' all the germs.

4. ELBONICS (el bon' iks) n. The actions of two people maneuvering for one arm rest in a movie theater or airplane.

5. FRUST (frust) n. The small line of debris that refuses to be swept onto the dust pan and keeps backing a person across the room until he finally decides to give up and sweep it under the rug.

6. LACTOMANGULATION (lak' to man guy lay' shun) n Manhandling the "open here" spout on a milk container so badly that one has to resort to the 'illegal' side.

7. PEPPIER (pehp ee ay') n. The waiter at a fancy restaurant whose sole purpose seems to be walking around asking diners if they want ground pepper.

8. PHONESIA (fo nee' zhuh) n. The affliction of dialing a phone number and forgetting whom you were calling just as they answer.

9. PUPKUS (pup'kus) n. The moist residue left on a window after a dog presses its nose to it.

10.TELECRASTINATION (tel e kras tin ay' shun) n. The act of always letting the phone ring at least twice before you pick it up, even when you're only six inches away.

11.DISHPANSATION: (dish pan say shun) N. The relief provided by a technician who has just repaired you automatic dishwasher.

Read This; It's Funny!!

Subject: New Dog Cross Breeds

The following breeds are now recognized by the AKC:

Collie + Lhasa Apso
Collapso, a dog that folds up for easy transport

Spitz + Chow Chow
Spitz-Chow, a dog that throws up a lot

Pointer + Setter
Poinsetter, a traditional Christmas pet

Great Pyrenees + Dachshund
Pyradachs, a puzzling breed

Pekingnese + Lhasa Apso
Peekasso, an abstract dog

Irish Water Spaniel + English Springer Spaniel
Irish Springer, a dog fresh and clean as a whistle

Labrador Retriever + Curly Coated Retriever
Lab Coat Retriever, the choice of research scientists

Newfoundland + Basset Hound
Newfound Asset Hound, a dog for financial advisors

Terrier + Bulldog
Terribull, a dog that makes awful mistakes

Bloodhound + Labrador
Blabador, a dog that barks incessantly

Malamute + Pointer
Moot Point, owned by...oh, well, it doesn't matter anyway

Collie + Malamute
Commute, a dog that travels to work

Deerhound + Terrier
Derriere, a dog that's true to the end

Bull Terrier + Shitzu
Oh, never mind....

Read This; It's Funny!!

Subject: Gender

What gender are they???

From the Washington Post Style Invitation, in which it was postulated that English should have male and female nouns, and readers were asked to assign a gender to a noun of their choice and explain their reason.

The best submissions:

ZIPLOC BAGS - male, because they hold everything in, but you can always see right through them.

SWISS ARMY KNIFE - male, because even though it appears useful for a wide variety of work, it spends most of its time just opening bottles.

KIDNEYS - female, because they always go to the bathroom in pairs.

SHOE - male, because it is usually unpolished, with its tongue hanging out.

COPIER - female, because once turned off, it takes a while to warm up. Because it is an effective reproductive device when the right buttons are pushed. Because it can wreak havoc when the wrong buttons are pushed.

TIRE - male, because it goes bald and often is over inflated.

HOT AIR BALLOON - male, because to get it to go anywhere you have to light a fire under it... and, of course, there's the hot air part.

SPONGES - female, because they are soft and squeezable and retain water.

WEB PAGE - female, because it is always getting hit on.

SUBWAY - male, because it uses the same old lines to pick people up.

HOURGLASS - female, because over time, the weight shifts to the bottom.

HAMMER - male, because it hasn't evolved much over the last 5,000 years, but it's handy to have around.

REMOTE CONTROL - female... Ha! You thought I'd say male. But consider, it gives man pleasure, he'd be lost without it, and while he doesn't always know the right buttons to push, he keeps trying.

Read This; It's Funny!!

Subject: Questions for the Wise

If lawyers are disbarred and clergymen defrocked, it follows that electricians can be delighted, musicians denoted, cowboys deranged, models deposed and dry cleaners depressed?

Laundry workers could decrease, eventually becoming depressed and depleted!

Even more, bed makers will be debunked, baseball players will be debased, landscapers will be deflowered, bulldozer operators will be degraded, organ donors will be delivered, software engineers will be detested, the BVD company will be debriefed, and even musical composers will eventually decompose.

On a more positive note though, perhaps we can hope politicians will be devoted.

Subject: Rules for Writers

1. Verbs HAS to agree with their subjects.
2. Prepositions are not words to end sentences with.
3. And don't start a sentence with a conjunction.
4. It is wrong to ever split an infinitive.
5. Avoid cliches like the plague. (They're old hat)
6. Also, always avoid annoying alliteration.
7. Be more or less specific.
8. Parenthetical remarks (however relevant) are (usually) unnecessary.
9. Also too, never, ever use repetitive redundancies.
10. No sentence fragments.
11. Contractions aren't necessary and shouldn't be used.
12. Foreign words and phrases are not apropos.
13. Do not be redundant; do not use more words than necessary; it's highly superfluous.
14. One should NEVER generalize.
15. Comparisons are as bad as cliches.
16. Don't use no double negatives.
17. Eschew ampersands & abbreviations, etc.
18. One-word sentences? Eliminate.
19. Analogies in writing are like feathers on a snake.
20. The passive voice is to be ignored.
21. Eliminate commas, that are, not necessary. Parenthetical words however should be enclosed in commas.
22. Never use a big word when a diminutive one would suffice.
23. Kill all exclamation points!!!
24. Use words correctly, irregardless of how others use them.
25. Understatement is always the absolute best way to put forth earth shaking ideas.
26. Use the apostrophe in it's proper place and omit it when its not needed.
27. Eliminate quotations. As Ralph Waldo Emerson said, "I hate quotations. Tell me what you know."
28. If you've heard it once, you've heard it a thousand times: Resist hyperbole; not one writer in a million can use it correctly.
29. Puns are for children, not groan readers.
30. Go around the barn at high noon to avoid colloquialisms.
31. Even IF a mixed metaphor sings, it should be derailed.
32. Who needs rhetorical questions?
33. Exaggeration is a billion times worse than understatement.

Read This; It's Funny!!

And finally...
34. Proofread carefully to see if you any words out.

Subject: Today's Stock Market Report

Helium was up, feathers were down.
Paper was stationary.
Fluorescent tubing was dimmed in light trading.
Knives were up sharply.
Cows steered into a bull market.
Pencils lost a few points.
Hiking equipment was trailing.
Elevators rose,
while escalators continued their slow decline.
Weights were up in heavy trading.
Light switches were off.
Mining equipment hit rock bottom.
Diapers remained unchanged.
Shipping lines stayed at an even keel.
The market for raisins dried up.
Coca Cola fizzled.
Caterpillar stock inched up a hill.
Sun peaked at midday.
Balloon prices were inflated.
Scott Tissue touched a new bottom.
And batteries exploded
in an attempt to recharge the market.

Read This; It's Funny!!

Subject: Weather by Degree

60 degrees - Californians put their sweaters on.
50 degrees - Miami residents turn on the heat.
45 degrees - Vermont residents go to outdoor concert.
40 degrees - You can see your breath.
                Californians shiver uncontrollably.
                Minnesotans go swimming.
35 degrees - Italian cars won't start.
32 degrees - Water freezes.
30 degrees - You plan your vacation in Australia.
25 degrees - Ohio water freezes.
                Californians weep pitiably.
                Minnesotans eat ice cream.
                Canadians go swimming.
20 degrees - Politicians begin to talk about the homeless.
                New York City water freezes.
                Miami residents plan vacation further south.
15 degrees - French cars don't start.
                Cat insists on sleeping in your bed with you.
10 degrees - You need jumper cables to get your car going.
 5 degrees - American cars won't start.
 0 degrees - Alaskans put on T-shirts.
-10 degrees - German cars don't start.
                Eyes freeze shut when you step outside.
-15 degrees - You can cut your breath and use it to build an
                igloo.
                Miami residents cease to exist.
-20 degrees - Cat insists on sleeping in pajamas with you.
                Politicians actually do something about the
                homeless.
                Minnesotans shovel snow off roof.
                Japanese cars don't start.
-25 degrees - Too cold to think.
                You need jumper cables to get the driver going.
-30 degrees - You plan a two week hot bath.
                Swedish cars don't start.
-40 degrees - Californians disappear.
                Minnesotans button their top button.
                Canadians put on sweater.
-50 degrees - Congressional hot air freezes.
                Alaskans close the bathroom window.

-80 degrees - Polar bears move south.
-90 degrees - Lawyers put their hands in their own pockets.
-100 degrees - Hell freezes over.

Read This; It's Funny!!

Subject: The Y1K Crisis

Canterbury, England. A.D. 999.

An atmosphere close to panic prevails today throughout Europe as the millennial year 1000 approaches, bringing with it the so-called "Y1K Bug," a menace which, until recently, hardly anyone had ever heard of. Prophets of doom are warning that the entire fabric of Western Civilization, based as it now is upon monastic computations, could collapse, and that there is simply not enough time left to fix the problem.

Just how did this disaster-in-the-making ever arise? Why did no one anticipate that a change from a three-digit to a four-digit year would throw into total disarray all liturgical chants and all metrical verse in which any date is mentioned? Every formulaic hymn, prayer, ceremony and incantation dealing with dated events will have to be rewritten to accommodate three extra syllables. All tabular chronologies with three-space year columns, maintained for generations by scribes using carefully hand-ruled lines on vellum sheets, will now have to be converted to four-space columns, at enormous cost. In the meantime, the validity of every official event, from baptisms to burials, from confirmations to coronations, may be called into question.

"We should have seen it coming ," says Brother Cedric of St. Michael Abbey, here in Canterbury. "What worries me most is that THOUSAND contains the word THOU, which occurs in nearly all our prayers, and of course always refers to God. Using it now in the name of the year will seem almost blasphemous, and is bound to cause terrible confusion. Of course, we could always use Latin, but that might be even worse — The Latin word for Thousand is Mille which is the same as the Latin for mile. We won't know whether we are talking about time or distance!"

Stonemasons are already reported threatening to demand a proportional pay increase for having to carve an extra numeral in all dates on tombstones, cornerstones and monuments. Together with its inevitable ripple effects, this alone could plunge the hitherto-stable medieval economy into chaos.

A conference of clerics has been called at Winchester to discuss the entire issue, but doomsayers are convinced that the matter is now one of personal survival. Many families, in expectation of the worst, are stocking up on holy water and indulgences.

128

Are You One?

Subject: Do You Have A.A.A.D.D? 130
Subject: You Know You're Not a Kid Anymore If 131
Subject: You Worked During the 90's If 132
Subject: You've Been Out of College Too Long When.... 134

Read This; It's Funny!!

Subject: Do You Have A.A.A.D.D?

I thought it would help to know there are others out there.
WE ARE NOT ALONE!!!!!

They have finally found a diagnosis for my condition.
Hooray!!

I have recently been diagnosed with A.A.A.D.D. !

Age Activated Attention Deficit Disorder...

This is how it goes: I decide to wash the car; I start toward
the garage and notice the mail on the table. Ok, I'm going to
wash the car. But first I'm going to go through the mail. I lay
the car keys down on the desk, discard the junk mail and I notice
the trash can is full. Ok, I'll just put the bills on my desk and
take the trash can out, but since I'm going to be near the mailbox
anyway, I'll pay these few bills first.

Now, where is my checkbook? Oops, there's only one check
left. My extra checks are in my desk. Oh, there's the coke I was
drinking. I'm going to look for those checks.

But first I need to put my coke further away from the
computer, oh maybe I'll pop it into the fridge to keep it cold for
a while. I head towards the kitchen and my flowers catch my
eye, they need some water. I set the coke on the counter and uh
oh! There are my glasses. I was looking for them all morning!
I'd better put them away first.

I fill a container with water and head for the flower pots - -
Aaaaaagh!

Someone left the TV remote in the kitchen. We'll never think
to look in the kitchen tonight when we want to watch television
so I'd better put it back in the family room where it belongs.

I splash some water into the pots and onto the floor, I throw
the remote onto a soft cushion on the sofa and I head back down
the hall trying to figure out what it was I was going to do?

End of Day: The car isn't washed, the bills are unpaid, the
coke is sitting on the kitchen counter, the flowers are half
watered, the checkbook still only has one check in it and I can't
seem to find my car keys! When I try to figure out how come
nothing got done today, I'm baffled because I KNOW I WAS
BUSY ALL DAY LONG!!!

I realize this is a serious condition and I'll get help,
BUT FIRST I think I'll check my e-mail...

Please send this to everyone you know because
I DON'T REMEMBER TO WHOM I'VE SENT THIS !!!

130

Subject: You Know You're Not a Kid Anymore If

1. You can live without sex but not without glasses.
2. Your back goes out more than you do.
3. You quit trying to hold your stomach in, no matter who walks into the room.
4. You buy a compass for the dash of your car.
5. You are proud of your lawn mower.
6. Your best friend is dating someone half their age ...and isn't breaking any laws.
7. You sing along with the elevator music.
8. You would rather go to work than stay home sick.
9. You constantly talk about the price of gasoline.
10. You enjoy hearing about other people's operations.
11. You consider coffee one of the most important things in life.
12. You make an appointment to see the dentist.
13. You no longer think of speed limits as a challenge.
14. Neighbors borrow your tools.
15. People call at 9 p.m. and ask, "Did I wake you?"
16. You answer a question with, "Because I said so!"
17. You send money to PBS.
18. The end of your tie doesn't come anywhere near the top of your pants.
19. You wear black socks with sandals.
20. You know what the word "equity" means.
21. You can't remember the last time you laid on the floor to watch television.
22. You talk about "good grass" and you're referring to someone's lawn.
23. You get into a heated argument about pension plans.
24. You got cable for the weather channel.
25. You have a party and the neighbors don't even realize it.

Read This; It's Funny!!

Subject: You Worked During the 90's If

You've sat at the same desk for 4 years and worked for 3 different organizations.

Your resume is in a diskette in your pocket.

You get really excited about a 2% pay raise.

You learn about your layoff on the news.

Your supervisor doesn't have the ability to do your job.

Salaries of the members on the Executive Board are higher than all the developing countries' gross national products combined.

It's dark when you drive to and from work.

Communication is something your section is having problems with.

You see a good looking person and know it is a visitor.

Free food left over from meetings is your main staple.

Being sick is defined as "can't walk" or "in the hospital."

You're already late on the work task you just got.

You work 200 hours for a $100 bonus check.

"Vacation" is something you roll over to next year, or a check you get every January.

Your relatives and family describe your job as "working with computers".

Your business cards are no longer correct just one month after you receive them.

You have every "Cup-A-Soup" brand known to man in your desk drawer.

You have no hobbies that do not involve an electronic device.

During any outside-of-work event that vaguely resembles a social activity, your co-workers outnumber your family members.

"Shopping" is something you do in the duty-free.

You must fill in your own job performance evaluations and target goals because no one else really knows what you do anyway. Besides, the HR Department was outsourced last month.

Your biggest loss from a system crash is that you've lost your best jokes.

You read this entire list and understood it.

Read This; It's Funny!!

Subject: You've Been Out of College Too Long When....

Your potted plants stay alive.

You keep more food than beer in the fridge.

You carry an umbrella.

You watch the Weather Channel.

You don't know what time Taco Bell closes anymore.

MTV News is no longer your primary source for information.

A $4.00 bottle of wine is no longer 'pretty good stuff'.

You actually eat breakfast foods at breakfast time.

Grocery lists are longer than: "macaroni & cheese, diet pepsi, Ho-ho's".

'I just can't drink the way I used to' replaces "I'm never going to drink that much again".

You don't get liquored up at home, to save money, before going to a bar.

You know you're old when you hear the words "Mickey's", "Old English", and "St Ives" and you shudder.

Dear Sir or Madam

Subject: Letter to a Bank 136
Subject: Letter to the IRS 139
Subject: Stewart to Bombeck 142

Read This; It's Funny!!

Subject: Letter to a Bank

Below is an actual letter sent to a Bank in the United States.

The Bank Manager thought it amusing enough to have it published in the New York Times.

Dear Sir:

I am writing to thank you for bouncing my check with which I endeavored to pay my plumber last month. By my calculations some three nanoseconds must have elapsed between his presenting the check and the arrival in my account of the funds needed to honor it. I refer, of course, to the automatic monthly deposit of my entire salary, and arrangement which, I admit, has only been in place for eight years.

You are to be commended for seizing that brief window of opportunity, and also for debiting my account by $50 by way of penalty for the inconvenience I caused to your bank.

My thankfulness springs from the manner in which this incident has caused me to rethink my errant financial ways. You have set me on the path of fiscal righteousness. No more will our relationship be blighted by these unpleasant incidents, for I am restructuring my affairs in 2003, taking as my model the procedures, attitudes and conduct of your very bank. I can think of no greater compliment and I know you will be excited and proud to hear it.

To this end, please be advised about the following changes:

I have noticed that whereas I personally attend to your telephone calls and letters, when I try to contact you, I am confronted by the impersonal, ever-changing, pre-recorded, faceless entity which your bank has become.

From now on I, like you, choose only to deal with a flesh-and-blood person.

My mortgage and loan repayments will, therefore and hereafter, no longer be automatic, but will arrive at your bank, by check, addressed personally and confidentially to an employee at your branch whom you must nominate.

You will be aware that it is an offense under the Postal Act for any other person to open such an envelope.

Please find attached an Application Contact Status Form which I require your chosen employee to complete. I am sorry it runs to eight pages, but in order that I know as much about him or her as your bank knows about me, there is no alternative.

Please note that all copies of his or her medical history must be countersigned by a Notary Public, and the mandatory details of his/her financial situation (income, debts, assets and liabilities) must be accompanied by documented proof.

In due course I will issue your employee with a PIN number which he/she must quote in dealings with me. I regret that it cannot be shorter than 28 digits but, again, I have modeled it on the number of button presses required to access my account balance on your phone bank service.

As they say, imitation is the sincerest form of flattery. Let me level the playing field even further by introducing you to my new telephone system, which you will notice, is very much like yours.

My Authorized Contact at your bank, the only person with whom I will have any dealings, may call me at any time and will be answered by an automated voice service:

Press buttons as follows:

1. To make an appointment to see me.
2. To query a missing payment.
3. To transfer the call to my living room, in case I am there.
4. To transfer the call to my bedroom, in case I am sleeping.
5. To transfer the call to my toilet,h in case I am attending to nature.
6. To transfer the call to my mobile phone if I am not at home.
7. To leave a message on my computer, a password to access my computer is required. Password will be communicated at a later date to the Authorized Contact.
8. To return to the main menu and to listen to options 1 through 7.
9. To make a general complaint or inquiry. The contact will then be put on hold, pending the attention of my automated answering service. While this may on occasion involve a lengthy wait, uplifting music will play for the duration of the call. This month I've chosen a refrain from "The Best of Woodie Guthrie:

"Oh, the banks are made of marble,
With a guard at every door,
And the vaults are filled with silver,
That the miners sweated for."

On a more serious note, we come to the matter of cost. As your bank has often pointed out, the ongoing drive for greater

Read This; It's Funny!!

efficiency comes at a cost which you have always been quick to pass on to me. Let me repay your kindness by passing some costs back.

First, there is a matter of advertising material you send me.

This I will read for a fee of $20 per page. Inquiries from the Authorized Contact will be billed at $5 per minute of my time spent in response. Any debits to my account, as, for example, in the matter of the penalty for the dishonored check, will be passed back to you.

My new phone service runs at 75 cents a minute. You will be well advised to keep your inquiries brief and to the point.

Regrettably, but again following your example, I must also levy an establishment fee to cover the setting up of this new arrangement.

May I wish you a happy, if ever-so-slightly less prosperous, New Year?

Your Humble Client

Henry T. Rodgerson
Climate Heating & Cooling

Subject: Letter to the IRS

Leave it to an accountant to come up with a funny story about the IRS.

Note: Sometimes a story comes along that needs no polishing or enhancement to make it better. This is one of those. It is a real letter submitted to the IRS, in the midst of 1995's weird and bizarre denial of dependents, exemptions and credits. The letter speaks for itself.

Dear Sirs:

I am responding to your letter denying the deduction for two of the three dependents I claimed on my 1994 Federal Tax return. Thank you. I have questioned whether or not these are my children for years. They are evil and expensive. It's only fair that, since they are minors and no longer my responsibility, the government should know something about them and what to expect over the next year. Please do not try to reassign them to me next year and reinstate the deduction. They are yours!

The oldest, Kristen, is now 17. She is brilliant. Ask her! I suggest you put her to work in your office where she can answer people's questions about their returns. While she has no formal training, it has not seemed to hamper her mastery of any subject you can name. Taxes should be a breeze. Next year she is going to college. I think it's wonderful that you will now be responsible for that little expense. While you mull that over, keep in mind that she has a truck. It doesn't run at the moment, so you have the choice of appropriating some Department of Defense funds to fix the vehicle, or getting up early to drive her to school. Kristen also has a boyfriend. Oh joy! While she possesses all of the wisdom of the universe, her alleged mother and I have felt it best to occasionally remind her of the virtues of abstinence, or in the face of overwhelming passion, safe sex. This is always uncomfortable, and I am quite relieved you will be handling this in the future. May I suggest that you reinstate Dr. Jocelyn Elders who had a rather good handle on the problem.

Patrick is 14. I've had my suspicions about this one. His eyes are a little closer together than those of normal people. He may be a tax examiner himself one day, if he is not incarcerated first. In February, I was awakened at three in the morning by a police officer who was bringing Pat home. He and his friends were TP'ing houses.

Read This; It's Funny!!

In the future, would you like him delivered to the local IRS office, or to Ogden, UT? Kids at 14 will do almost anything on a dare. His hair is purple. Permanent dye, temporary dye, what's the big deal? Learn to deal with it. You'll have plenty of time, as he is sitting out a few days of school after instigating a food fight in the cafeteria. I'll take care of filing your phone number with the vice-principal. Oh yes, he and all of his friends have raging hormones. This is the house of testosterone and it will be much more peaceful when he lives in your home. DO NOT leave him or his friends unsupervised with girls, explosives, flammables, inflatables, vehicles, or telephones. (They find telephones a source of unimaginable amusement. Be sure to lock out the 900 and 976 numbers!)

Heather is an alien. She slid through a time warp and appeared as if by magic one year. I'm sure this one is yours. She is 10 going on 21. She came from a bad trip in the sixties. She wears tie-dyed clothes, beads, sandals, and hair that looks like Tiny Tim's. Fortunately you will be raising my taxes to help offset the pinch of her remedial reading courses. "Hooked On Phonics" is expensive, so the schools dropped it. But here's the good news! You can buy it yourself for half the amount of the deduction that you are denying me! It's quite obvious that we were terrible parents (ask the other two). She cannot speak English. Most people under twenty understand the curious patois she fashioned out of valley girls/boys in the hood/reggae/yuppie/political double speak. The school sends her to a speech pathologist who has her roll her "r's". It added a refreshing Mexican/Irish touch to her voice. She wears hats backwards, baggy pants, and wants one of her ears pierced four more times. There is a fascination with tattoos that worries me, but I am sure that you can handle it. Bring a truck when you come to get her, she sort of "nests" in her room and I think that it would be easier to move the entire thing than find out what it is really made of.

You denied two of the three exemptions, so it is only fair that you get to pick which two you will take. I prefer that you take the youngest two, I will still go bankrupt with Kristen's college, but then I am free! If you take the two oldest, then I still have time for counseling before Heather becomes a teenager. If you take the two girls, then I won't feel so bad about putting Patrick in a military academy.

140

Dear Sir or Madam

Please let me know of your decision as soon as possible, as I have already increased the withholding on my W-4 to cover the $395 in additional tax and made a down payment on an airplane.

Yours truly,
Bob
(Note: The IRS allowed the deductions and reinstated his refund.)

Read This; It's Funny!!

Subject: Stewart to Bombeck

Martha Stewart's Christmas letter to Erma Bombeck:

Dearest Erma,

This perfectly delightful note is being sent on paper I made myself to tell you what I have been up to.

Since it snowed last night, I got up early and made a sled with old barn wood and a glue gun.

I hand painted it in gold leaf, got out my loom, and made a blanket in peaches and mauves.

Then to make the sled complete, I made a white horse to pull it from DNA that I had just sitting around in my craft room.

By then, it was time to start making the place mats and napkins for my twenty breakfast guests. I'm serving the old standard Stewart twelve-course breakfast, but I'll let you in on a little secret: I didn't have time to make the tables and chairs this morning, so I used the ones I had on hand.

Before I moved the table into the dining room, I decided to add just a touch of the holidays so I repainted the room in pinks and stenciled gold stars on the ceiling. Then while the homemade bread was rising, I took antique candle molds and made the dishes exactly the same shade of pink to use for breakfast. These were made from Hungarian clay, which you can get at almost any Hungarian craft store.

Well, I must run. I need to finish the buttonholes on the dress I'm wearing for breakfast.

I'll get out the sled and drive this note to the post office as soon as the glue dries on the envelope I'll be making. Hope my breakfast guests don't stay too long... I have 40,000 cranberries to string with bay leaves before my speaking engagement at noon. It's a good thing.

Love,
Martha Stewart

P.S. When I made the ribbon for this typewriter, I used 1/8-inch gold gauze. I soaked the gauze in a mixture of white grapes and blackberries which I grew, picked, and crushed last week just for fun.

Dear Sir or Madam

Response from Erma Bombeck:

HI Martha,

I'm writing this on the back of an old shopping list. Pay no attention to the coffee and jelly stains. I'm twenty minutes late getting my daughter up for school, packing a lunch with one hand and on the phone with the dog pound (seems old Ruff needs bailing out again).

Burnt my arm on the curling iron when I was trying to make those cute curly fries. How DO they do that? Still can't find the scissors to cut out some snowflakes. I tried using an old disposable razor but trashed the tablecloth.

Tried that cranberry thing. The frozen cranberries mushed up after I defrosted them in the microwave. Oh, and don't use Fruity Pebbles as a substitute in that Rice Krispies snowball recipe unless you happen to like a disgusting shade that resembles puke!

The smoke alarm is going off. Talk to ya later.

Love,

Erma

On Being Married

Subject: Behind Every Great Inventor 145
Subject: Buy It! 146
Subject: Fore!!! 148
Subject: Heart to Heart 149
Subject: What's in the Box 150
Subject: To Be Six, Again 151
Subject: Marriage Quotes 152

Subject: Behind Every Great Inventor

The inventor spent many long years at work in his laboratory,
  but not everyone, it appears, knows the rest of the story.

For uncounted hours he toiled each night as he struggled
  to invent an electric light.

But tonight, at last, as you may have guessed,
  the time was right for its very first test.

He worked without ceasing or thought of a letup,
  and with trembling fingers, he adjusted the setup.

Each step in his mind he calmly rehearsed
  as he hoped for the best while fearing the worst.

'Twas the moment of truth as he turned the lamp on.
  It burst into light - the darkness was gone.

The relief in his heart we can safely assume
  as its glorious brilliance flooded the room.

In the flush of triumph, he happily rested
  but found his patience sorely tested,

As he heard the voice he had come to dread,
  "TURN OFF THAT LIGHT, TOM, AND COME TO BED!"

Read This; It's Funny!!

Subject: Buy It!

There are several men in the locker room of a private club after exercising. Suddenly a cell phone that was on one of the benches rings. A man picks it up and the following conversation ensues:

Hello?

Honey, It's me.

Sugar!

Are you at the club?

Yes.

Great! I am at the mall 2 blocks from where you are. I saw a beautiful mink coat... It is absolutely gorgeous!! Can I buy it?

What's the price?

Only $1,500.00

Well, OK, go ahead and get, if you like it that much...

Uhhh and I also stopped by the Mercedes dealership and saw the 2003 models. I saw one I really liked. I spoke with the salesman and he gave me a really good price ... and since we need to exchange the BMW that we bought last year.....

What price did he quote you?

Only $60,000...

OK, but for that price I want it with all the options.

Great!, before we hang up, something else...

What?

It might look like a lot, but I was reconciling your bank account and... I stopped by the real estate agent this morning and I saw the house we had looked at last year ... it's on sale!! Remember? The one with a pool, English Garden, acre of park area, beachfront property...

How much are they asking?

Only $450,000... a magnificent price, and I see that we have that much in the bank to cover...

Well, than go ahead and buy it, but just bid $420,000. OK?

OK, sweetie... Thanks! I'll see you later!! I love you!!!

Bye... I do too...

The man hangs up, closes the phone's flap and raises his hand while holding the phone and asks to all those present:

"Does anyone know who this phone belongs to?"

Read This; It's Funny!!

Subject: Fore!!!

A man staggers into an emergency room with a concussion, multiple bruises, two black eyes and a five iron wrapped tightly around his throat.

Naturally, the doctor asks him what happened.

"Well, it was like this," said the man. "I was having a quiet round of golf with my wife, when at a difficult hole, we both sliced our balls into a pasture of cows. We went to look for them, and while I was rooting around noticed one of the cows had something white at its rear end.

I walked over and lifted up the tail, and sure enough, there was a golf ball with my wife's monogram on it—stuck right in the middle of the cow's butt! That's when I made my big mistake."

"What did you do?" asks the doctor.

"Well, I lifted the cow's tail and yelled to my wife, 'Hey, this looks like yours!'."

I don't remember much after that."

Subject: Heart to Heart

Her husband had been slipping in and out of a coma for several months, yet she had stayed by his bedside every single day.

One day, when he came to, he motioned for her to come nearer.

As she sat by him, he whispered, eyes full of tears, "You know what? You have been with me all through the bad times...When I got fired, you were there to support me. When my business failed, you were there. When my parents were killed, you were by my side. When we lost the house, you stayed right here. When my health started failing, you were still by my side, and now that I am dying, you are still here....You know what?"

"What dear?" She gently asked, smiling as her heart began to fill with warmth.

"I think you bring me bad luck."

Read This; It's Funny!!

Subject: What's in the Box

As a new bride, Aunt Edna moved into the small home on her husband's ranch near Snowflake. She put a shoe box on a shelf in her closet and asked her husband never to touch it. For fifty years Uncle Jack left the box alone, until Aunt Edna was old and dying. One day when he was putting their affairs in order, he found the box again and thought it might hold something important. Opening it, he found two doilies and $82,500 in cash.

He took the box to her and asked about the contents. "My mother gave me that box the day we married," she explained. "She told me to make a doily to help ease my frustrations every time I got mad at you." Uncle Jack was very touched that in 50 years she'd only been mad at him twice.

"What's the $82,500 for?" he asked.

"Oh, that's the money I made selling the doilies."

Subject: To Be Six, Again

A man asked his wife what she'd like for her birthday.

"I'd love to be, uhm, six again," she replied.

On the morning of her birthday, he got her up bright and early and off they went to a local theme park. What a day! He put her on every ride in the park: the Death Slide, the Screaming Loop, the Wall of Fear, everything there was! Wow! Five hours later she staggered out of the theme park, her head reeling and her stomach upside down.

Right to a McDonald's they went, where her husband ordered her a Big Mac along with extra fries and a refreshing chocolate shake.! Then it was off to a movie — the latest epic, and hot dogs, popcorn, Pepsi Cola and M&Ms.

What a fabulous adventure! Finally she wobbled home with her husband and collapsed into bed.

He leaned over and lovingly asked, "Well, dear, what was it like being six again?"

One eye opened. "You idiot! ....I meant my dress size."

The moral of this story: Even when a man is listening, he's still gonna get it wrong.

Read This; It's Funny!!

Subject: Marriage Quotes

To keep your marriage brimming,
With love in the loving cup
Whenever you're wrong, admit it;
Whenever you're right, shut up.
—OGDEN NASH, "A word to Husbands"

Marriage is like pantyhose. It all depends on what you put into
it.
—PHYLLIS SCHLAFLY

If you want to sacrifice the admiration of many men for the
criticism of one, go ahead and get married!
—KATHARINE HOUGHTON HEPBURN

In every house of marriage, there's room for an interpreter.
—STABKET JYBUTZ Route Six

Love is so much better when you are not married.
—MARIA CALLAS (attributed)

Love is an ideal thing, marriage is a real thing; a confusion of
the real with the ideal never goes unpunished.
—JOHANN WOLFGANG VON GOETHE

One should always be in love. That is the reason one should not
marry.
—OSCAR WILDE

Anyone who is repelled by his sweetheart's farts has no business
talking about love.
—GUNTER GRASS

Men and Women

Subject: Because I'm A Guy 154
Subject: Differences Between a Man and a Woman 156
Subject: Discoveries of the Sexes 157
Subject: How-to Classes For Men 158
Subject: Moods of a Woman 160
Subject: Open Letter to Women 161
Subject: Raging River 163
Subject: On the Next Edition of "Survivor" 164
Subject: Top Ten 165
Subject: Why It's Great to be a Man... 166
Subject: Perfection 168
Subject: Young King Arthur 169
Subject: Tech Support 171

Read This; It's Funny!!

Subject: Because I'm A Guy

Because I'm a guy, I must hold the television remote control in my hand while I watch TV. If the thing has been misplaced, I'll miss a whole show looking for it, though one time I was able to survive by holding a calculator.

Because I'm a guy, when I lock my keys in the car I will fiddle with a wire clothes hanger and ignore your suggestions that we call a road service until long after hypothermia has set in. Oh, and when the car isn't running very well, I will pop the hood and stare at the engine as if I know what I'm looking at. If another guy shows up, one of us will say to the other, "I used to be able to fix these things, but now with all these computers and everything, I wouldn't know where to start." We will then drink beer.

Because I'm a guy, when I catch a cold I need someone to bring me soup and take care of me while I lie in bed and moan. You never get as sick as I do, so for you this isn't an issue.

Because I'm a guy, I can be relied upon to purchase basic groceries at the store, like milk, or bread. I cannot be expected to find exotic items like "Cumin" or "Tofu." For all I know these are the same thing. And never, under any circumstances, expect me to pick up anything for which "feminine hygiene product" is a euphemism.

Because I'm a guy, when one of our appliances stops working I will insist on taking it apart, despite evidence that this will just cost me twice as much once the repair person gets here and has to put it back together.

Because I'm a guy, I don't think we're all that lost, and no, I don't think we should stop and ask someone. Why would you listen to a complete stranger—how the heck could HE know where we're going?

Because I'm a guy, there is no need to ask me what I'm thinking about. The answer is always either sex or football, though I have to make up something else when you ask, so don't.

Because I'm a guy, I do not want to visit your mother, or have your mother come visit us, or talk to her when she calls, or think about her any more than I have to. Whatever you got her for mother's day is ok, I don't need to see it. Did you remember to pick up something for my mom, too?

Because I'm a guy, I am capable of announcing, "one more beer and I really have to go," and mean it every single time I say it, even when it gets to the point that the one bar closes and my buddies and I have to go hunt down another. I will find it increasingly hilarious to have my pals call you to tell you I'll be home soon, and no, I don't understand why you threw all my clothes into the front yard. What's the connection?

Because I'm a guy, you don't have to ask me if I liked the movie. Chances are, if you're crying at the end of it, I didn't.

Because I'm a guy, yes, I have to turn up the radio when Bruce Springsteen or The Doors comes on, and then, yes, I have to tell you every single time about how Bruce had his picture on the cover of Time and Newsweek the same day, or how Jim Morrison is buried in Paris and everyone visits his grave. Please do not behave as if you do not find this fascinating.

Because I'm a guy, I think what you're wearing is fine. I thought what you were wearing five minutes ago was fine, too. Either pair of shoes is fine. With the belt or without it looks fine. Your hair is fine. You look fine. Can we just go now?

Because I'm a guy and this is, after all, the new millennium, I will share equally in the housework. You do the laundry, the cooking, the cleaning, and the dishes. I'll do the rest.

Read This; It's Funny!!

Subject: Differences Between a Man and a Woman

1. A man will pay $2 for a $1 item he wants.
   A woman will pay $1 for a $2 item that she doesn't want.

2. A woman worries about the future until she gets a husband.
   A man never worries about the future until he gets a wife.

3. A successful man is one who makes more money than his wife can spend.
   A successful woman is one who can find such a man.

4. To be happy with a man you must understand him a lot & love him a little.
   To be happy with a woman you must love her a lot & not try to understand her at all.

5. Married men live longer than single men - but married men are a lot more willing to die.

6. Any married man should forget his mistakes - there's no use in two people remembering the same thing.

7. Men wake up as good-looking as they went to bed.
   Women somehow deteriorate during the night.

8. A woman marries a man expecting he will change, but he doesn't.
   A man marries a woman expecting that she won't change & she does.

9. A woman has the last word in any argument.
   Anything a man says after that is the beginning of a new argument.

10. There are 2 times when a man doesn't understand a woman - before marriage & after marriage.

Subject: Discoveries of the Sexes

Man discovered weapons, invented hunting.
Woman discovered hunting, invented furs.

Man discovered colors, invented painting.
Woman discovered painting, invented make-up.

Man discovered speech, invented conversation.
Woman discovered conversation, invented gossip.

Man discovered agriculture, invented food.
Woman discovered food, invented diet.

Man discovered friendship, invented love.
Woman discovered love, invented marriage.

Man discovered woman, invented sex.
Woman discovered sex, invented headache.

Man discovered trade, invented money.
Woman discovered money, and man was a complete mess after that.

Read This; It's Funny!!

Subject: How-to Classes For Men

Note: These are classes for men offered at the local Adult Learning Center.

Due to the complexity and difficulty level of their content, each course will accept a maximum of 8 participants.

Topic 1: How to fill up the ice cube trays.
 Step by step, with slide presentation.

Topic 2: The toilet paper roll: Do they grow on the holders?
Roundtable discussion.

Topic 3: Is it possible to urinate using the technique of lifting the seat up and avoiding the floor/walls and nearby bathtub?
Group practice.

Topic 4: Fundamental differences between the laundry hamper and the floor.
Pictures and explanatory graphics.

Topic 5: The after-dinner dishes and silverware: Can they levitate and fly into the kitchen sink?
Examples on video.

Topic 6: Loss of identity: Losing the remote to your significant other.
Help-line support and support groups.

Topic 7: Learning how to find things, starting with looking in the right place instead of turning the house upside down while screaming.
Open forum.

Topic 8: Health watch: Bringing her flowers is not harmful to your health.
Graphics and audio tape.

Topic 9: Real men ask for directions when lost.
Real life Testimonials.

Topic 10: Is it genetically impossible to sit quietly as she parallel parks?
Driving simulation.

Topic 11: Learning to live: Basic differences between mother and wife.
On-line class and role playing.

Topic 12: How to be the ideal shopping companion:
Relaxation exercises, meditation, and breathing techniques.

Topic 13: How to fight cerebral atrophy: Remembering birthdays, anniversaries, other important dates and calling when you're going to be late.
Cerebral shock therapy sessions and full lobotomies offered.

NOTE:
Upon completion of the course, diplomas will be issued to the survivors.

Read This; It's Funny!!

Subject: Moods of a Woman

An angel of truth and a dream of fiction,
A woman is a bundle of contradiction,
She's afraid of a wasp, will scream at a mouse,
But will tackle a stranger alone in the house.
Sour as vinegar, sweet as a rose,
She'll kiss you one minute, then turn up her nose,
She'll win you in rage, enchant you in silk,
She'll be stronger than brandy, milder than milk;
At times she'll be vengeful, merry and sad,
She'll hate you like poison, and love you like mad.

MOODS OF A MAN
Hungry
Horny
Sleepy

160

Subject: Open Letter to Women

Consider this an open letter to all women, all ages, all races, all shapes and sizes, married or single.

Dear Ladies,

1. Learn to work the toilet seat. If it's up, put it down. We need it up, you need it down. You don't hear us complaining about you leaving it down.
2. If you won't dress like the Victoria's Secret girls, don't expect us to act like soap opera guys.
3. If you think you're fat, you probably are. Don't ask us. We refuse to answer.
4. Don't cut your hair. Ever. Long hair is always more attractive than short hair. One of the big reasons guys fear getting married is that married women always cut their hair, and by then you're stuck with her.
5. Birthdays, Valentines, and Anniversaries are not quests to see if we can find the perfect present yet again!
6. If you ask a question you don't want an answer to, expect an answer you don't want to hear.
7. Sometimes, we're not thinking about you. Live with it. Don't ask us what we're thinking about unless you are prepared to discuss such topics as hunting and fishing, NFL formation, or monster trucks.
8. Sunday = Sports. It's like the full moon or the changing of the tides. Let it be.
9. Shopping is not a sport, and no, we're never going to think of it that way.
10. When we have to go somewhere, absolutely anything you wear is fine. Really. You have enough clothes. You have too many shoes.
11. Crying is blackmail.
12. Ask for what you want. Let's be clear on this one: Subtle hints don't work. Strong hints don't work. Really obvious hints don't work. Just say it!
13. No, we don't know what day it is. We never will. Mark anniversaries on the calendar.
14. Peeing standing up is more difficult. We're bound to miss sometimes.

Read This; It's Funny!!

15. Most guys own three pairs of shoes. What makes you think we'd be any good at choosing which pair, out of thirty, would look good with your dress?

16. Yes, and No are perfectly acceptable answers to almost every question. Come to us with a problem only if you want help solving it. That's what we do.

17. Sympathy is what your girlfriends are for.

18. A headache that lasts for 17 months is a problem. See a doctor.

19. Foreign films are best left to foreigners.

20. Check your oil.

21. It is neither in your best interest nor ours to take the quiz together. No, it doesn't matter which quiz.

22. Anything we said 6 months ago is inadmissible in an argument. All comments become null and void after 7 days.

23. If something we said can be interpreted two ways, and one of the ways makes you sad or angry, we meant the other one.

24. Let us ogle. We're going to look anyway; it's genetic.

25. You can either tell us to do something OR tell us how to do something but not both.

26. Whenever possible, please say whatever you have to say during commercials.

27. ALL men see in only 16 colors. Peach is a fruit, not a color.

28. If it itches, it will be scratched.

29. Beer is as exciting for us as handbags are for you.

30. If we ask what's wrong and you say "nothing," we will act like nothing's wrong. We know you're lying, but it's just not worth the hassle.

31. What is a doily?

Subject: Raging River

One day three men were hiking and unexpectedly came upon a large raging, violent river. They needed to get to the other side, but had no idea of how to do so. . The first man prayed to God, saying, "Please God, give me the strength to cross this river."

Poof! God gave him big arms and strong legs, and he was able to swim across the river in about two hours, after almost drowning a couple of times.

Seeing this, the second man prayed to God, saying, "Please God, give me the strength ..and the tools to cross this river." Poof! God gave him a rowboat and he was able to row across the river in about an hour, after almost capsizing the boat a couple of times.

The third man had seen how this worked out for the other two, so he also prayed to God saying, "Please God, give me the strength and the tools...and the intelligence... to cross this river." And poof! God turned him into a woman. She looked at the map, hiked upstream a couple of hundred yards, then walked across the bridge. . . SEND THIS TO A SMART WOMAN WHO NEEDS A LAUGH AND TO THE GUYS YOU THINK CAN HANDLE IT!

Read This; It's Funny!!

Subject: On the Next Edition of "Survivor"

Six married men will be dropped on an island with one car and four kids each, for six weeks.

Each kid plays two sports and either takes music or dance classes.

There is no access to fast food.

Each man must take care of his four kids, keep his assigned house clean, correct all homework, complete science projects, cook, do laundry, etc.

The men only have access to television when the kids are asleep, and all chores are done. There is only one TV between them, and there is no remote.

The men must shave their legs and wear makeup daily, which they must apply themselves, either while driving or while making four lunches.

They must attend weekly PTA meetings; clean up after their sick children at 3:00 a.m.; make an Indian hut model with six toothpicks, a tortilla and one marker; and get a four-year-old to eat a serving of peas.

The kids vote them off the island, based on performance. The last man wins only if he has enough energy to be intimate with his spouse at a moment's notice.

If the last man does win, he can play the game over and over again for the next 18 to 25 years, eventually earning the right to be called "Mother".

Subject: Top Ten

Top Ten Things Men Understand about Women

1.
2.
3.
4.
5.
6.
7.
8.
9.
10.

Just smile and pass it on!

Read This; It's Funny!!

Subject: Why It's Great to be a Man...

You can kill your own food

Phone conversations last only 30 seconds

You know lots of useful stuff about tanks and airplanes

A five day vacation requires only one suitcase

Bathroom lines are 80% shorter

You can open all your own jars

Old friends don't care if you've lost or gained weight

When clicking through the channels you don't have to stop on every shot of someone crying

You can go to the bathroom alone

Your last name stays put

You can leave a hotel room bed unmade

The garage is all yours

You get extra credit for the slightest act of thoughtfulness

You see the humor in "Terms of Endearment"

You can be showered and ready in 10 minutes

Wedding plans take care of themselves

If someone forgets to invite you to something, they can still be your friend

Your underwear costs $7.50 for a pack of 3

None of your coworkers have the power to make you cry

You don't have to shave below your neck

You don't have to curl up next to some big, hairy guy every night

If you're 34 and single, no one notices

Chocolate is just another snack

You can quietly enjoy a car ride from the passenger seat

Flowers and/or Duct Tape fix everything

You never have to worry about anyone else's feelings

Three pair of shoes are more than enough

You can say anything and not worry about what people think

You can whip your shirt off on a hot day

Car mechanics tell you the truth

You don't care if someone doesn't notice your new haircut

You can watch a game in silence for hours without your buddy thinking "He must be mad at me"

One mood, all the time, 24/7

You can admire Clint Eastwood without having to starve yourself to look like him

Gray hair and wrinkles add character

Wedding dress $2,000 — Tux rental $85 bucks

You don't care if someone is talking behind your back

You don't pass on the dessert and then mooch off someone else's

The remote is yours and yours alone

You need not pretend you're "freshening up" when you go to the bathroom

If you don't call your buddy when you said you would, he won't tell your friends that you've "changed"

If another guy shows up at the party in the same outfit, you might become lifelong buddies

The occasional well-rendered belch is expected

If something mechanical didn't work, you can bash it with a hammer and throw it across the room

New shoes don't cut, blister, or mangle your feet

You think the idea of punting that small, ankle-biting dog is funny

If you retain water, it is in a canteen

Flushing the toilet is optional

Read This; It's Funny!!

Subject: Perfection

Once upon a time, a perfect man and a perfect woman met. After a perfect courtship, they had a perfect wedding. Their life together was, of course, perfect. One snowy, stormy Christmas Eve, this perfect couple was driving their perfect car along a winding road, when they noticed someone at the side of he road in distress.

Being the perfect couple, they stopped to help.

There stood Santa Claus with a huge bundle of toys. Not wanting to disappoint any children on the eve of Christmas, the perfect couple loaded Santa and his toys into their vehicle. Soon they were driving along delivering the toys.

Unfortunately, the driving conditions deteriorated and the perfect couple and Santa Claus had an accident. Only one of them survived the accident.

Question: Who was the survivor?
(Scroll down for the answer. Trust me, it's worth it)

Answer: The perfect woman survived. She's the only one who really existed in the first place. Everyone knows there is no Santa Claus and there is no such thing as a perfect man.

**** Women stop reading here, that is the end of the story.

**** Men keep scrolling.

So, if there is no perfect man and no Santa Claus, the woman must have been driving. This explains why there was a car accident.

By the way, if you're a woman and you're still reading, this illustrates another point: Women never listen.

Subject: Young King Arthur

Remember the moral of this story and take heed!!!

Young King Arthur was ambushed and imprisoned by the monarch of a neighboring kingdom. The monarch could have killed him, but was moved by Arthur's youthful happiness. So he offered him freedom, as long as he could answer a very difficult question. Arthur would have a year to figure out the answer; if, after a year, he still had no answer, he would be killed. The question was:

What do women really want?

Such a question would perplex even the most knowledgeable man, and, to young Arthur, it seemed an impossible query. Well, since it was better than death, he accepted the monarch's proposition to have an answer by year's end.

He returned to his kingdom and began to poll everybody: the princess, the prostitutes, the priests, the wise men, the court jester. In all, he spoke with everyone but no one could give him a satisfactory answer. What most people did tell him was to consult the old witch, as only she would know the answer. The price would be high, since the witch was famous throughout the kingdom for the exorbitant prices she charged. The last day of the year arrived and Arthur had no alternative but to talk to the witch. She agreed to answer his question, but he'd have to accept her price first: The old witch wanted to marry Gawain, the most noble of the Knights of the Round Table and Arthur's closest friend! Young Arthur was horrified: she was hunchbacked and awfully hideous, had only one tooth, smelled like sewage water, often made obscene noises... He had never run across such a repugnant creature. He refused to force his friend to marry her and have to endure such a burden. Gawain, upon learning of the proposal, spoke with Arthur. He told him that nothing was too big of a sacrifice compared to Arthur's life and the preservation of the Round Table. Hence, their wedding was proclaimed, and the witch answered Arthur's question: What a woman really wants is to be able to be in charge of her own life. Everyone instantly knew that the witch had uttered a great truth and that Arthur's life would be spared. And so it went. The neighboring monarch spared Arthur's life and granted him total freedom.

Read This; It's Funny!!

What a wedding Gawain and the witch had! Arthur was torn between relief and anguish. Gawain was proper as always, gentle and courteous. The old witch put her worst manners on display. She ate with her hands, belched and farted, and made everyone uncomfortable. The wedding night approached: Gawain, steeling himself for a horrific night, entered the bedroom. What a sight awaited! The most beautiful woman he'd ever seen lay before him!

Gawain was astounded and asked what had happened. The beauty replied that since he had been so kind to her (when she'd been a witch), half the time she would be her horrible, deformed self, and the other half, she would be her beautiful maiden self. Which would he want her to be during the day and which during the night? What a cruel question!

Gawain began to think of his predicament: During the day a beautiful woman to show off to his friend, but at night, in the privacy of his home, an old spooky witch? Or would he prefer having by day a hideous witch, but by night a beautiful woman to enjoy many intimate moments?

What would you do?

What Gawain chose follows below, but don't read until you've made your own choice.

Noble Gawain replied that he would let her choose for herself. Upon hearing this, she announced that she would be beautiful all the time, because he had respected her and had let her be in charge of her own life.

What is the moral of this story?

THE MORAL IS THAT IT DOESN'T MATTER IF YOUR WOMAN IS PRETTY OR UGLY, UNDERNEATH IT ALL, SHE'S STILL A WITCH.

Or...

IF YOUR WOMAN DOESN'T GET HER OWN WAY, THINGS ARE GOING TO GET UGLY!

170

Subject: Tech Support

A letter from a newlywed to Technical Support. it helps if you read it as if you were talking about versions of Computer Programs.

Dear Tech Support,

Last year I upgraded from Boyfriend 5.0 to Husband 1.0 and noticed a slow down in the overall performance, particularly in the flower and jewelry applications that had operated flawlessly under Boyfriend 5.0.

In addition, Husband 1.0 uninstalled many other valuable programs, such as Romance 9.5 and Personal Attention 6.5, but installed undesirable programs such as NFL 5.0 and NBA 3.0. And now Conversation 8.0 no longer runs, and House Cleaning 2.6 simply crashes the system. I've tried running Nagging 5.3 to fix these problems, but to no avail.

What can I do?

Sincerely,
Desperate

Reply: Dear Desperate:

First, keep in mind that Boyfriend 5.0 is an entertainment package, while Husband 1.0 is in operating system. Try entering the command C:\I THOUGHT YOU LOVED ME and download Tears 6.2 to install Guilt 3.0.

If all works as designed, Husband 1.0 should then automatically run the applications Jewelry 2.0 and Flowers 3.5. But remember, overuse can cause Husband 1.0 to default to Grumpy Silence 2.5, Happy Hour 7.0 or Beer 6.1.

Beer 6.1 is a very bad program that will create Snoring Loudly.Wav files. Whatever you do, DO NOT install Mother-in-Law 1.0 or re-install another Boyfriend program. These are not supported applications and will crash Husband 1.0.

In summary, Husband 1.0 is a great program, but it does have a limited memory and cannot learn new applications quickly. You might consider additional software to improve memory and hard drive performance.

I personally recommend Hot Food 3.0 and Lingerie 6.9.

Good luck, !!!

Quips

Subject: Airlines 173
Subject: Mutterings 175
Subject: Exercise is Good For You... 176
Subject: Birthdays and Time 177
Subject: Life Quips 178
Subject: Little Hints and Sayings 179
Subject: More Wisdom 181
Subject: Politically Correct Ways to Call Someone Stupid . 182
Subject: Some Things For You to Ponder............................. 183
Subject: Ponder This 2 184
Subject: Sarcastic Remarks to Get You Through the Day .. 186
Subject: Still More Quips 188
Subject: Useful Conflict Resolution Phrases 189
Subject: Wisdom of Will Rogers 190
Subject: Words of Wisdom 191

Subject: Airlines

Occasionally, airline attendants make an effort to make the "in-flight safety lecture" a bit more entertaining. Here are some real examples that have been heard or reported:

"As we prepare for takeoff, please make sure your tray tables and seat backs are fully upright in their most uncomfortable position."

"There may be 50 ways to leave your lover, but there are only 4 ways out of this airplane..."

"Your seat cushions can be used for floatation, and in the event of an emergency water landing, please take them with our compliments."

"We do feature a smoking section on this flight; if you must smoke, contact a member of the flight crew and we will escort you to the wing of the airplane."

"Smoking in the lavatories is prohibited. Any person caught smoking in the lavatories will be asked to leave the plane immediately."

"Good morning. As we leave Dallas, it's warm, the sun is shining, and the birds are singing. We are going to Charlotte, where it's dark, windy and raining. Why in the world y'all wanna go there I really don't know."

Pilot - "Folks, we have reached our cruising altitude now, so I am going to switch the seat belt sign off. Feel free to move about as you wish, but please stay inside the plane till we land... it's a bit cold outside, and if you walk on the wings it affects the flight pattern."

And, after landing: "Thank you for flying Delta Business Express. We hope you enjoyed giving us the business as much as we enjoyed taking you for a ride."

Read This; It's Funny!!

As we waited just off the runway for another airliner to cross in front of us, some of the passengers were beginning to retrieve luggage from the overhead bins. The head steward announced on the intercom, "This aircraft is equipped with a video surveillance system that monitors the cabin during taxiing. Any passengers not remaining in their seats until the aircraft comes to a full and complete stop at the gate will be strip-searched as they leave the aircraft."

As the plane landed and was coming to a stop at Washington National, a lone voice comes over the loudspeaker: "Whoa, big fella... WHOA"

Here are a few heard from Northwest:

"Should the cabin lose pressure, oxygen masks will drop from the overhead area. Please place the bag over your own mouth and nose before assisting children or adults acting like children."

"As you exit the plane, please make sure to gather all of your belongings. Anything left behind will be distributed evenly among the flight attendants. Please do not leave children or spouses."

And from the pilot during his welcome message:

"We are pleased to have some of the best flight attendants in the industry... Unfortunately none of them are on this flight!"

Subject: Mutterings

1. I can please only one person per day. Today is not your day. Tomorrow, isn't looking good either.
2. I love deadlines. I especially like the whooshing sound they make as they go flying by.
 3. Am I getting smart with you? How would you know?
 4. I'd explain it to you, but your brain would explode.
 5. Someday we'll look back on all this and plow into a parked car.
 6. There are very few personal problems that cannot be solved through a suitable application of high explosives.
 7. Tell me what you need, and I'll tell you how to get along without it.
 8. Accept that some days you're the pigeon, and some days you're the statue.
 9. Needing someone is like needing a parachute. If he isn't there the first time you need him, chances are you won't be needing him again.
10. I don't have an attitude problem. You have a perception problem.
11. Last night I lay in bed looking up at the stars in the sky and I thought to myself, "Where the heck is the ceiling?!"
12. My Reality Check bounced.
13. On the keyboard of life, always keep one finger on the escape key.
14. I don't suffer from stress. I'm a carrier.
15. You're slower than a herd of turtles stampeding through peanut butter.
16. Do not meddle in the affairs of dragons, 'cuz, like, you are crunchy and taste good with ketchup.
17. Everybody is somebody else's weirdo.
18. Never argue with idiots. They drag you down to their level then beat you with experience.

Read This; It's Funny!!

Subject: Exercise is Good For You...

1) My grandmother started walking five miles a day when she was 60. She's 97 now and we don't know where the heck she is.
2) I joined a health club last year, spent about 400 bucks. Haven't lost a pound. Apparently you have to show up.
3) The only reason I would take up jogging is so that I could hear heavy breathing again.
4) I have to exercise in the morning before my brain figures out what I'm doing.
5) I don't exercise at all. If God meant for us to touch our toes, he would have put them further up our body.
6) I like long walks, especially when they are taken by people who annoy me.
7) I have flabby thighs, but fortunately my stomach covers them.
8) The advantage of exercising every day is that you die healthier.
9) If you are going to try cross-country skiing, start with a small country.
10) I don't jog. It makes the ice jump right out of my glass.

Subject: Birthdays and Time

Birthdays are nature's way of telling us to eat more cake.

Forget about the past, you can't change it.
Forget about the future, you can't predict it.
Forget about the present, I didn't get you one.

Start every day with a smile and get it over with.
  —W.C. Fields

Time flies like an arrow. Fruit flies like a banana.

I intend to live forever — so far, so good!

Don't worry about temptation — as you grow older, it starts avoiding you.

Age is something that doesn't matter, unless you are a cheese.

He is so old that his blood type was discontinued.

I guess I don't so much mind being old, as I mind being fat and old.
Peter Gabriel

Read This; It's Funny!!

Subject: Life Quips

1) No one is listening until you make a mistake.
2) Never test the depth of the water with both feet.
3) If you haven't had much education, you must use your brain.
4) The things that come to those who wait are the things that those who got there first left behind.
5) Some days you're the bug, some days you're the windshield.
6) It's better to be the windshield.
7) Before criticizing anyone you should walk a mile in their shoes. That way, when you criticize them, you're a mile away and you'll have their shoes.
8) If Barbie is so popular, why do you have to buy her friends?
9) The problem with the gene pool is that there is no lifeguard.
10) An "expert" is someone from out of town carrying a clipboard.
11) The journey of a thousand miles begins with a broken fan belt or leaky tire.
12) If you think nobody cares if you're alive, try missing a couple of car payments.
13) Never ask a barber if he thinks you need a haircut.
14) It may be that your sole purpose in life is to serve as a warning to others.
15) If you lend somebody $20 and never see that person again, it was probably worth it.
16. Errors have been made. Others will be blamed.

Subject: Little Hints and Sayings

Blessed are those who hunger and thirst, for they are sticking to their diets.

Life is an endless struggle full of frustrations and challenges, but eventually you find a hairstylist you like.

The reason why women over fifty don't have babies: They'd only put them down and forget where they left them.

One of the life's mysteries is how a two pound box of candy can make a woman gain five pounds.

It's frustrating when you know all the answers, but, nobody bothers to ask you the questions.

The real art of conversation is not only to say the right thing in the right place, but also to leave unsaid the wrong thing at the tempting moment.

Time may be a great healer, but it's also a lousy beautician.

Brain cells come and brain cells go, but fat cells live forever.

Age doesn't always bring wisdom. Sometimes age comes alone.

Life not only begins at forty, it begins to show.

Just when I was getting used to yesterday, along came today.

Sometimes I think I understand everything, then I regain consciousness.

If at first you don't succeed, see if the loser gets anything.

You don't stop laughing because you grow old; you grow old because you stop laughing.

I don't mind the rat race, but I could do with a little more cheese.

Age is important, only if you're cheese or wine.

Read This; It's Funny!!

I had to give up jogging for my health. My thighs kept rubbing together and setting my pantyhose on fire.
Amazing! You just hang something in your closet for a while, and it shrinks two sizes.

It is bad to suppress laughter; it goes back down and spreads to your hips.

The only time a woman wishes she were a year older is when she is pregnant.

Freedom of the press means no-iron clothes.

Inside some of us is a thin person struggling to get out, but they can usually be sedated with a few pieces of chocolate cake.

Subject: More Wisdom

God grant me the senility to forget the people I never liked anyway, the good fortune to run into the ones I do, and the eyesight to tell the difference.

Now that I'm older, here's what I've discovered: I started out with nothing, I still have most of it.

All reports are in. Life is now officially unfair.

If all is not lost, where is it?

Some days you're the dog, some days you're the hydrant.

I wish the buck stopped here. I sure could use a few ...

Kids in the back seat cause accidents; accidents in the back seat cause kids.

It's hard to make a comeback when you haven't been anywhere.

When you're finally holding all the cards, why does everyone else decide to play chess?

It's not hard to meet expenses ... they're everywhere.

Old programmers never die. They just terminate and stay resident.

A day without sunshine is like a day in Seattle.

Jury: Twelve people who determine which client has the better attorney.

Read This; It's Funny!!

Subject: Politically Correct Ways to Call Someone Stupid

A few clowns short of a circus
A few fries short of a happy meal
An experiment in artificial stupidity
A few beers short of a six pack
Dumber than a box of hair
Doesn't have all his cornflakes in one box
The wheel's spinning but the hamster's dead
Not the coldest beer in the fridge
One Fruit Loop shy of a full bowl
All foam, no beer
Has an IQ of 2 but it takes 3 to grunt
Couldn't pour water out of a boot with instructions on the heel
An intellect rivaled only by garden tools
Has the IQ of a house plant
As smart as bait
Chimney's clogged
Elevator doesn't go all the way to the top floor
His antenna doesn't pick up all the channels
Proof that evolution can go in reverse
Not the sharpest tool in the shed
The lights are on but no-one's home
The light at the end of the tunnel has been extinguished
2 sticks short of a bundle
A few pints short of a quart
Cables connected, no voltage
Swimming in the shallow end of the gene pool
One neuron short of a synapse

Subject: Some Things For You to Ponder...

1. Don't sweat the petty things, and don't pet the sweaty things.
2. One tequila, two tequila, three tequila, floor.
3. One nice thing about egotists: They don't talk about other people.
4. To be intoxicated is to feel sophisticated but not be able to say it.
5. Never underestimate the power of stupid people in large groups.
6. The older you get, the better you realize you were.
7. I doubt, therefore I might be.
8. Age is a very high price to pay for maturity.
9. Procrastination is the art of keeping up with yesterday.
10. Women like silent men, they think they're listening.
11. Men are from earth. Women are from earth. Deal with it.
12. Give a man a fish and he will eat for a day. Teach him how to fish, and he will sit in a boat and drink beer all day.
13. A fool and his money are soon partying.
14. Do pediatricians play miniature golf on Wednesdays?
15. Before they invented drawing boards, what did they go back to?
16. Do infants enjoy infancy as much as adults enjoy adultery?
17. If all the world is a stage, where is the audience sitting?
18. If one synchronized swimmer drowns, do the rest have to drown too?
19. If the #2 pencil is the most popular, why is it still #2?
20. If work is so terrific, how come they have to pay you to do it?
21. If you ate pasta and antipasta, would you still be hungry?
22. If you try to fail, and succeed, which have you done?

****
23. I am at one with my duality.
****

Read This; It's Funny!!

Subject: Ponder This 2

How can you tell when you run out of invisible ink?

Could someone ever get addicted to counseling? If so, how could you treat them?

Can you be a closet claustrophobic?

Did Adam and Eve have navels?

Does anyone ever vanish with a trace?

How does the guy who drives the snowplow get to work in the mornings?

If a turtle doesn't have a shell, is he homeless or naked?

If a chronic liar tells you he is a chronic liar do you believe him?

If a mute child swears, does his mother wash his hands with soap?

If a tree falls in the forest and no one is around to see it, do the other trees make fun of it?

If all those psychics know the winning lottery numbers, why are they all still working?

If nothing ever sticks to TEFLON, how do they make TEFLON stick to the pan?

If olive oil comes from olives, where does baby oil come from?

What would a chair look like if your knees bent the other way?

If pro is the opposite of con, is progress the opposite of congress?

If quitters never win, and winners never quit, who came up with, "Quit while you're still ahead?"

What did we do before the Law of Gravity was passed?

184

If the Energizer Bunny attacks someone, is it charged with battery?

If you have a bunch of odds and ends and get rid of all but one of them, what do you call it?

What happens if you get scared half to death twice?

Why are we afraid of falling? Shouldn't we be afraid of the sudden stop?

Why do airlines call flights nonstop? Don't they all stop eventually?

Why is the alphabet in that order?

Why isn't "phonetic" spelled the way it sounds?

You know how most packages say "Open here?" What is the protocol if the package says, "Open somewhere else?"

Sooner or later, doesn't EVERYONE stop smoking?

How do you know when it's time to tune your bagpipes?

Read This; It's Funny!!

Subject: Sarcastic Remarks to Get You Through the Day

1. And your crybaby whiny-assed opinion would be...?
2. Do I look like a stupid people person?
3. This isn't an office. It's Hell with fluorescent lighting.
4. I started out with nothing & still have most of it left.
5. I pretend to work. They pretend to pay me.
6. Sarcasm is just one more service we offer.
7. If I throw a stick, will you leave?
8. You!... Off my planet!
9. If I want to hear the pitter patter of little feet, I'll put shoes on my cats.
10. Does your train of thought have a caboose?
11. Did the aliens forget to remove your anal probe?
12. A PBS mind in an MTV world.
13. Allow me to introduce my selves.
14. Whatever kind of look you were going for, you missed.
15. Suburbia: where they tear out the trees & then name streets after them.
16. Well, this day was a total waste of makeup.
17. See no evil, hear no evil, date no evil.
18. Are those your eyeballs? I found them in my cleavage.
19. I'm not your type. I'm not inflatable.
20. Not all men are annoying. Some are dead.
21. Did I mention the kick in the groin you'll be receiving if you touch me?
22. I'm trying to imagine you with a personality.
23. A cubicle is just a padded cell without a door.
24. Stress is when you wake up screaming & you realize you haven't fallen asleep yet.
25. Can I trade this job for what's behind door 1?
26. I thought I wanted a career, turns out I just wanted paychecks.
27. Okay, okay, I take it back! UnF**k you!
28. Too many freaks, not enough circuses.
29. Macho Law prohibits me from admitting I'm wrong.
30. Nice perfume. Must you marinate in it?
31. Chaos, panic, & disorder - my work here is done.
32. I plead contemporary insanity.
33. And which dwarf are you?
34. How do I set a laser printer to stun?

 A train stops at a train station, a car stops at a service station, and on my desk I have a work station ...

Read This; It's Funny!!

Subject: Still More Quips

Everyone has a photographic memory. Some don't have film

Save the whales. Collect the whole set.

A day without sunshine is like, ... night.

Diplomacy is saying "nice doggy" until you find a rock.

On the other hand, you have different fingers.

Change is inevitable, except from a vending machine.

Back up my hard drive? How do I put it in reverse?

I just got lost in thought. It was unfamiliar territory

When the chips are down, the buffalo is empty.

Seen it all, done it all, can't remember most of it.

Those who live by the sword get shot by those who don't.

I feel like I'm diagonally parked in a parallel universe.

He's not dead, he's electroencephalographically challenged.

You have the right to remain silent. Anything you say will be misquoted, then used against you.

I wonder how much deeper would the ocean be without sponges.

Honk if you love peace and quiet.

Despite the cost of living, have you noticed how it remains so popular?

Nothing is foolproof to a sufficiently talented fool.

Atheism is a non-profit organization.

Subject: Useful Conflict Resolution Phrases

1. Thank you. We're all refreshed and challenged by your unique point of view.
2. The fact that no one understands you doesn't mean you're an artist.
3. I don't know what your problem is, but I'll bet it's hard to pronounce.
4. Any connection between your reality and mine is purely coincidental.
5. I have plenty of talent and vision. I just don't care.
6. I like you. You remind me of when I was young and stupid.
7. What am I? Flypaper for freaks!?
8. I'm not being rude. You're just insignificant.
9. I'm already visualizing the duct tape over your mouth.
10. I will always cherish the initial misconceptions I had about you.
11. It's a thankless job, but I've got a lot of Karma to burn off.
12. Yes, I am an agent of Satan, but my duties are largely ceremonial.
13. No, my powers can only be used for good.
14. How about never? Is never good for you?
15. I'm really easy to get along with once you people learn to worship me.
16. You sound reasonable...Time to up my medication.
17. I'll try being nicer if you'll try being smarter.
18. I'm out of my mind, but feel free to leave a message...
19. I don't work here. I'm a consultant.
20. Who me? I just wander from room to room.
21. My toys! My toys! I can't do this job without my toys!
22. It might look like I'm doing nothing, but at the cellular level I'm really quite busy.
23. At least I have a positive attitude about my destructive habits.
24. You are validating my inherent mistrust of strangers.
25. I see you've set aside this special time to humiliate yourself in public.
26. Someday, we'll look back on this, laugh nervously and change the subject.

Read This; It's Funny!!

Subject: Wisdom of Will Rogers

1. "Lettin' the cat outta the bag is a whole lot easier than puttin' it back in."
2. "If you're riding ahead of the herd, take a look back every now and then to make sure it's still there."
3. "If you get to thinking you're a person of some influence, try ordering somebody else's dog around."
4. "After eating an entire bull, a mountain lion felt so good he started roaring. He kept it up until a hunter came along and shot him... The moral: When you're full of bull, keep your mouth shut."
5. "Never kick a cow chip on a hot day."
6. "There's two theories to arguing with a woman. Neither one works."
7. "If you find yourself in a hole, the first thing to do is stop digging."
8. "Never slap a man who's chewing tobacco."
9. "It doesn't take a genius to spot a goat in a flock of sheep."
10. "The quickest way to double your money is to fold it over and put it back in your pocket."
11. "Don't squat with your spurs on."
12. "Good judgment comes from experience, and a lot of that comes from bad judgment."
13. "Never miss a good chance to shut up."
14. "Always drink upstream from the herd."
15. "When you're throwing' your weight around, be ready to have it thrown around by somebody else."
16. "When I die, I want to die like my grandfather who died peacefully in his sleep. Not screaming like all the passengers in his car."
17. "When you give a lesson in meanness to a critter or a person, don't be surprised if they learn their lesson. "

REMEMBER —For every minute you are angry with someone, you lose 60 seconds of happiness that you can never get back.

190

Subject: Words of Wisdom

I live in my own little world, but it's ok, they know me here.

I saw a woman wearing a sweatshirt with 'Guess' on it. I said, "Thyroid problem?"

I don't do drugs anymore 'cause I find I get the same effect just by standing up really fast.

Dyslexia means never having to say that you're yrros.

Regular naps prevent old age... especially if you take them while driving.

I don't approve of political jokes... I've seen too many of them get elected.

I have learned there is little difference in husbands, you might as well keep the first.

There are two sides to every divorce: Yours and dirt bag's.

If life deals you lemons, make lemonade; if it deals you tomatoes, make Bloody Mary's.

I was on a date recently, and the guy took me horseback riding. That was kind of fun, until we ran out of quarters.

I married my wife for her looks...but not the ones she's been giving me lately!

The next time you feel like complaining, remember: Your garbage disposal probably eats better than thirty percent of the people in this world.

Snowmen fall from Heaven unassembled.

Every time I walk into a singles bar I can hear Mom's wise words: "Don't pick that up, you don't know where it's been.

Old Humor

Subject: Found Money 193
Subject: Benefits of Being a Senior 194
Subject: Getting Old 196
Subject: Car Jacker 197
Subject: Senior Driver 198
Subject: Those People from Maine 199
Subject: Leonard and the Devil 200
Subject: I'm a Senior Citizen 201
Subject: Wisdom From Senior Citizens 203
Subject: Sharing Everything 205

Subject: Found Money

An elderly couple who were childhood sweethearts had married and settled down in their old neighborhood and are celebrating their fiftieth wedding anniversary. They walk down the street to their old school. There, they hold hands as they find the old desk they'd shared and where he had carved "I love you, Sally."

On their way back home, a bag of money falls out of an armored car practically at their feet. She quickly picks it up, but they don't know what to do with it, so they take it home. There, she counts the money, and it's fifty thousand dollars.

The husband says, "We've got to give it back."

She says, "Finders keepers", puts the money back in the bag, and hides it up in their attic.

The next day, two FBI men are going door-to-door in the neighborhood looking for the money and show up at their home. They say, "Pardon me, but did either of you find any money that fell out of an armored car yesterday?"

She says, "No."

The husband says, "She's lying. She hid it up in the attic."

She says, "Don't believe him, he's getting senile."

But the agents sit the man down and begin to question him. One says, "Tell us the story from the beginning."

The old man says, "Well, when Sally and I were walking home from school yesterday..."

The FBI guy looks at his partner and says, "Let's get out of here."

Read This; It's Funny!!

Subject: Benefits of Being a Senior

1. Kidnappers are not very interested in you.
2. In a hostage situation you are likely to be released first.
3. No one expects you to run into a burning building.
4. People no longer view you as a hypochondriac.
5. There is nothing left to learn the hard way.
6. Things you buy now won't wear out.
7. You can eat dinner at 4 PM.
8. You can live without sex but not without glasses.
9. You no longer think of speed limits as a challenge.
10. You quit trying to hold your stomach in, no matter who walks into the room.
11. Your eyes won't get much worse.
12. Your investment in health insurance is finally beginning to pay off.
13. Your joints are a more accurate meteorologist than the national weather service.
14. Your secrets are safe with your friends because they can't remember them either.
15. Your supply of brain cells is finally down to a manageable size.
16. You can't remember who sent you this list.

Chapter 1: SIGNS OF MENOPAUSE

1. You sell your home heating system at a yard sale.
2. Your husband jokes that instead of buying a wood stove, he is using you to heat the family room this winter. Rather than just saying you are not amused, you shoot him.
3. You have to write post-it notes with your kids' names on them.
4. The phenobarbital dose that wiped out the Heaven's Gate Cult gave you four hours of decent rest.
5. You change your underwear after every sneeze.
6. You're on so much estrogen that you take your Brownie troop on a field trip to Chippendale's.

194

Chapter 2: SIGNS OF WEAR

"OLD" IS WHEN.. Your sweetie says, "Let's go upstairs and make love, " and you answer, "Pick one, I can't do both!"

"OLD" IS WHEN.. Your friends compliment you on your new alligator shoes but you're barefoot.

"OLD" IS WHEN.. A sexy babe catches your fancy and your pacemaker opens the garage door.

"OLD" IS WHEN.. Going bra-less pulls all the wrinkles out of your face.

"OLD" IS WHEN.. You don't care where your spouse goes, just as long as you don't have to go along.

"OLD" IS WHEN.. You are cautioned to slow down by the doctor instead of by the police.

"OLD" IS WHEN.. "Getting a little action" means I don't need to take any fiber today.

"OLD" IS WHEN.. "Getting lucky" means you find your car in the parking lot.

"OLD" IS WHEN.. An "all-nighter" means not getting up to pee.

Read This; It's Funny!!

Subject: Getting Old

Signs You Are Getting Old

1. Your potted plants are alive. And you can't smoke any of them.

2. You keep more food than beer in the fridge.

3. You hear your favorite song on an elevator.

4. You're the one calling the police because those darn kids next door don't know how to turn down the stereo.

5. Your car insurance goes down and your car payments go up.

6. You feed your dog Science Diet instead of McDonald's.

7. Sleeping on the couch makes your back hurt.

8. You no longer take naps from noon to 6 p.m.

9. Dinner and a movie - The whole date instead of the beginning of one.

10. Eating a basket of chicken wings at 3 a.m. would severely upset, rather than settle, your stomach.

11. A $4.00 bottle of wine is no longer 'pretty good stuff.'

12. You actually eat breakfast foods at breakfast time.

13. "I just can't drink the way I used to," replaces "I'm never going to drink that much again."

14. Over 90% of the time you spend in front of a computer is for real work.

15. You read this entire list looking for one sign that doesn't apply to you!

Subject: Car Jacker

An elderly lady did her shopping and upon return, found four males in her car. She dropped her shopping bags and drew her handgun, proceeding to scream at them at the top of her voice that she knows how to use it and that she will if required: so get out of the car. The four men didn't wait around for a second invitation but got out and ran like mad, whereupon the lady proceeded to load her shopping bags into the back of the car and get into the drivers seat. Small problem, her key wouldn't fit the ignition.

Her car was identical and parked four or five spaces farther down.

She loaded her bags into her car and drove to the police station. The sergeant to whom she told the story nearly tore himself in two with laughter and pointed to the other end of the counter, where four pale white males were reporting a car jacking by a mad elderly white woman; no charges were filed.

Read This; It's Funny!!

Subject: Senior Driver

Sitting on the side of the highway waiting to catch speeding drivers, a State Police Officer sees a car puttering along at 22 MPH.

He thinks to himself, "This driver is just as dangerous as a speeder!" So he turns on his lights and pulls the driver over.

Approaching the car, he notices that there are five old ladies - two in the front seat and three in the back - wide-eyed and white as ghosts. The driver, obviously confused, says to him, "Officer, I don't understand, I was doing exactly the speed limit! What seems to be the problem?"

"Ma'am," the officer replies, "you weren't speeding, but you should know that driving slower than the speed limit can also be a danger to other drivers."

"Slower than the speed limit? No sir, I was doing the speed limit exactly...Twenty-two miles an hour!" the old woman says a bit proudly.

The State Police Officer, trying to contain a chuckle explains to her that "22" was the route number, not the speed limit.

A bit embarrassed, the woman grinned and thanked the officer for pointing out her error.

"But before I let you go, Ma'am, I have to ask...is everyone in this car OK? These women seem awfully shaken and they haven't muttered a single peep this whole time." The officer said.

"Oh, they'll be all right in a minute officer. We just got off Route 119".

Subject: Those People from Maine

Stumpy Grinder and his wife Martha were from Portland, Maine. Every year they went to the Portland Fair, and every year Stumpy said, "Ya know Mahtha, I'd like ta get a ride in that theah aihplane." Every year Martha would say, "I know Stumpy, but that aihplane ride costs ten dollahs... and ten dollahs is ten dollahs."

This year Stumpy says, "By Jeebers Mahtha, I'm 71 yeahs old, and if I don't go this time I may nevah go. Martha replies, "Stumpy, that theah aihplane ride is ten dollahs...and ten dollahs is ten dollahs."

But the pilot overhears them and says, "Folks, I'll make you a deal. I'll take you both up for a ride. If you can stay quiet for the entire ride and not say ONE word, I won't charge you. But just one word and it's ten dollars."

They agree and up they go...the pilot does all kinds of twists, turns, rolls, and dives, but not a word is heard. He does it one more time...still nothing... so he lands.

He turns to Stumpy as they come to a stop and says, "By golly, I did everything I could think of to get you to holler out, but you didn't."

And Stumpy replies, "Well, I was gonna say something when Mahtha fell out...but ten dollahs is ten dollahs!"

Read This; It's Funny!!

Subject: Leonard and the Devil

One bright, beautiful Sunday morning, everyone in the tiny town of Johnstown got up early and went to the local church. Before the services started, the townspeople were sitting in their pews and talking about their lives, their families, etc.

Suddenly, the Devil himself appeared at the front of the church. As you might imagine, everyone started screaming and running for the front entrance, trampling each other in a frantic effort to get away from evil incarnate.

Soon everyone was evacuated from the Church, except for one elderly gentleman named Leonard who sat calmly in his pew, not moving, seemingly oblivious to the fact that God's ultimate enemy was in his presence.

Now this confused Satan a bit, so he walked up to the man and said, "Don't you know who I am?"

Leonard replied, "Yep, sure do."

Satan asked, "Aren't you afraid of me?"

"Nope, sure ain't," said the man.

Satan was a little perturbed at this and queried, "Why aren't you afraid of me?"

The man calmly replied, "Been married to your sister for over 53 years."

Subject: I'm a Senior Citizen

I'm the life of the party, even if it lasts until 8 P.M.

I'm very good at opening childproof caps with a hammer.

I'm usually interested in going home before I get to where I'm going.

I'm the first one to find the bathroom wherever I go.

I'm awake many hours before my body allows me to get up.

I'm smiling all the time because I can't hear a word you are saying.

I'm very good at telling stories...over and over and over and over.

I'm aware that other people's grandchildren are not as bright as mine are.

I'm not grouchy; I just don't like traffic, waiting, crowds, children, and politicians.

I'm positive I did housework correctly before my mate retired.

I'm sure everything l can't find is in a secure place.

I'm realizing that aging is not for sissies.

I'm a walking storeroom of facts. I've just misplaced the storeroom.

I'm in the initial stage of my golden years: SS, CDs, IRA'S and AARP.

I'm having trouble remembering simple words like_____

I'm sure they are making adults much younger these days.

I'm wrinkled, sagging, and lumpy, and that's just my left leg.

Read This; It's Funny!!

I'm supporting all movements now. By eating bran, prunes, and raisins.

I'm so cared for: long term care, eye care, private care and dental.

I'm going to reveal what goes on behind closed doors....Absolutely nothing.

I'm a senior citizen and I think I'm having the time of my life!

Subject: Wisdom From Senior Citizens

1. When did my wild oats turn to prunes and all bran?

2. I finally got my head together, now my body is falling apart.

3. Funny, I don't remember being absent minded.

4. It is easier to get older than it is to get wiser.

5. If at first you do succeed, try not to look astonished.

6. A closed mouth gathers no feet.

7. I tried to get a life once, But they told me they were out of stock.

8. I went to school to become a wit, only got halfway though.

9. It was so different before everything changed.

10. Nostalgia isn't what it use to be.

11. It's not the pace of life that concerns me, it's the sudden stop at the end.

12. It's hard to make a comeback when you haven't been anywhere.

13. The only time the world beats a path to your door is if your in the bathroom.

14. Never knock on death's door, ring the bell and run (he hates that).

15. Lead me not into temptation (I can find the way myself).

16. If you are living on the edge, make sure your wearing your seat belt.

17. There are two kinds of pedestrians. The quick and the dead.

Read This; It's Funny!!

18. An unbreakable toy is useful for breaking other toys.

19. Health is merely the slowest possible rate at which one can die.

20. The only difference between a rut and a grave is the depth.

Subject: Sharing Everything

The little old couple walked slowly into McDonalds that cold winter evening. They looked out of place amid the young families and young couples eating there that night. Some of the customers looked admiringly at them.

You could tell what the admirers were thinking. "Look, there is a couple who has been through a lot together, probably for 60 years or more!"

The little old man walked right up to the cash register, placed his order with no hesitation and then paid for their meal. The couple took a table near the back wall and started taking food off of the tray. There was one hamburger, one order of french fries and one drink.

The little old man unwrapped the plain hamburger and carefully cut it in half. He placed one half in front of his wife. Then he carefully counted out the french fries, divided them in two piles and neatly placed one pile in front of his wife. He took a sip of the drink, his wife took a sip and then set the cup down between them.

As the man began to eat his few bites of hamburger the crowd began to get restless. Again you could tell what they were thinking. "That poor old couple. All they can afford is one meal for the two of them." As the man began to eat his french fries one young man stood and came over to the old couples table. He politely offered to buy another meal for the old couple to eat. The old man replied that they were just fine. They were used to sharing everything.

Then the crowd noticed that the little old lady hadn't eaten a bite. She just sat there watching her husband eat and occasionally taking turns sipping the drink. Again the young man came over and begged them to let him buy them something to eat. This time the lady explained that no, they were used to sharing everything together.

As the little old man finished eating and was wiping his face neatly with a napkin the young man could stand it no longer. Again he came over to their table and offered to buy some food. After being politely refused again he finally asked a question of the little old lady. "Maam, why aren't you eating. You said that you share everything. What is it that you are waiting for?"

She answered, "The teeth".

Jocks Slaps

Subject: Baseball In Heaven? 207
Subject: Golf 208
Subject: Priorities 209
Subject: Sports Geniuses 210

Subject: Baseball In Heaven?

Two buddies, Bob and Earl, were two of the biggest baseball fans in America. For their entire adult lives, Bob and Earl discussed baseball history in the winter and they poured over every box score during the baseball season. They went to 60 games a year. They even agreed that the one that died first would try to come back and tell the other if there was baseball in heaven.

One summer night, Bob passed away in his sleep after watching a Yankee victory earlier in the evening. Being that he was a big Yankee fan, he died a happy man.

A few nights later, his buddy Earl awoke to the sound of Bob's voice from beyond.

"Bob is that you?" Earl asked.

"Of course it is me," Bob replied.

"This is unbelievable!" Earl exclaimed. "So tell me, is there baseball in heaven?"

"Well I have some good news and some bad news for you. Which do you want to hear first?"

"Tell me the good news first."

"Well, the good news is that, yes, there is baseball in heaven, Earl."

"Oh, that is wonderful! So what could possibly be the bad news?"

"You're pitching tomorrow night."

Read This; It's Funny!!

Subject: Golf

Shortly after Pope John Paul II apologized to the nation of Israel for the treatment of Jews by the Catholic Church over the years, the leader of Israel sent back a message to the College of Cardinals. The proposal was for a friendly game of golf to be played between the two leaders or their representatives to show the friendship and ecumenical spirit shared by the Catholic and Jewish faiths.

The Pope met with his College of Cardinals to discuss the proposal.

"Your holiness," said one of the cardinals, "the reason Israel wants to challenge you to a game of golf to show that you are old and unable to compete. I am afraid that this would tarnish our image to the world."

The Pope thought about this and as he had never held a golf club in his life asked, "Don't we have a cardinal to represent me?"

"None that plays golf very well," a cardinal replied. "But," he added, "there is a man named Jack Nicklaus, an American golfer who is a devout Catholic. We can offer to make him a cardinal, then ask him to play against Israel's golfer as your personal representative. In addition to showing our spirit of cooperation, we'll also win the match."

Everyone agreed it was a great idea. The call was made. Of course, Nicklaus was honored and agreed to play as a representative of the pope.

The day after the match, Nicklaus reported to the Vatican to inform the pope of the result. "I have some good news and some bad news, Your Holiness," said the golfer.

"Tell me the good news, Cardinal Nicklaus," said the pope.

"Well, Your Holiness, I don't like to brag, but even though I've played some pretty terrific rounds of golf in my life, this was the best I have ever played, by far. I must have been inspired from above. My drives were long and true, my irons were accurate and purposeful and my putting was perfect. With all due respect, my play was truly miraculous."

"How can there be bad news?" the pope asked.

Nicklaus sighed, "I lost to Rabbi Tiger Woods by three strokes."

208

Subject: Priorities

Super Bowl Tix

Bob won a ticket to the Super Bowl. Approaching the stadium, he was extremely excited. Once he got inside, he couldn't find his seat. Finally he asked an usher to help him find his seat. The usher guided him to the top row. Then the usher pointed and said seat 25. Bob settled in his seat, and noticed he was almost as far from the field as possible. He pulled out a pair of binoculars, and could still barely make out the numbers on the players. He then gazed around the audience. He suddenly stopped as he came to a open seat in the first row. Bob packed up, and headed to his destination.

Upon arriving he saw an old man, sitting by himself. Bob then asked "Is this seat open?"

"Sure, sit down. No one is sitting there."

Bob was excited "Who would be crazy enough not to use a seat like this?"

"I am." said the man. "My wife and I have come to every Super Bowl since 1968."

"Where is she now?"

"She's dead."

"I am so sorry to hear......wasn't there a really close friend, or family member you could have invited?"

"Nope, they're all at the funeral."

Read This; It's Funny!!

Subject: Sports Geniuses

Chicago Cubs outfielder Andre Dawson on being a role model: "I want all the kids to do what I do, to look up to me. I want all the kids to copulate me."

New Orleans Saint RB George Rogers when asked about the upcoming season: "I want to rush for 1,000 or 1,500 yards, whichever comes first."

And, upon hearing Joe Jacoby of the 'Skins say "I'd run over my own mother to win the Super Bowl," Matt Millen of the Raiders said, "To win, I'd run over Joe's mom too."

Football commentator and former player Joe Theismann 1996: "Nobody in football should be called a genius. A genius is a guy like Norman Einstein."

Senior basketball player at the University of Pittsburgh: "I'm going to graduate on time, no matter how long it takes."

Bill Peterson, a Florida State football coach: "You guys line up alphabetically by height." And, "You guys pair up in groups of three, then line up in a circle."

Clemson recruit Ray Forsythe, who was ineligible as a freshman because of academic requirements: "I play football. I'm not trying to be a professor. The tests don't seem to make sense to me, measuring your brain on stuff I haven't been through in school."

Boxing promoter Dan Duva on Mike Tyson hooking up again with promoter Don King: "Why would anyone expect him to come out smarter? He went to prison for three years, not Princeton."

Stu Grimson, Chicago Blackhawks left wing, explaining why he keeps a color photo of himself above his locker: "That's so when I forget how to spell my name, I can still find my @#%#%@ clothes."

Shaquille O'Neal on whether he had visited the Parthenon during his visit to Greece: "I can't really remember the names of the clubs that we went to."

210

Shaquille O'Neal, on his lack of championships: "I've won at every level, except college and pro."

Lou Duva, veteran boxing trainer, on the Spartan training regime of heavyweight Andrew Golota: "He's a guy who gets up at six o'clock in the morning regardless of what time it is."

Pat Williams, Orlando Magic general manager, on his team's 7-27 record: "We can't win at home. We can't win on the road. As general manager, I just can't figure out where else to play." (1992)

Chuck Nevitt, North Carolina State basketball player, explaining to Coach Jim Valvano why he appeared nervous at practice: "My sister's expecting a baby, and I don't know if I'm going to be an uncle or an aunt."

Tommy Lasorda , Dodger manager, when asked what terms Mexican-born pitching sensation Fernando Valenzuela might settle for in his upcoming contract negotiations: "He wants Texas back." (1981)

Darrell Royal, Texas football coach, asked if the abnormal number of Longhorn injuries that season resulted from poor physical conditioning: "One player was lost because he broke his nose. How do you go about getting a nose in condition for football?" (1966)

Mike McCormack, coach of the hapless Baltimore Colts after the team's co-captain, offensive guard Robert Pratt, pulled a hamstring running onto the field for the coin toss against St. Louis: "I'm going to send the injured reserve players out for the toss next time." (1981)

Steve Spurrier, Florida football coach, telling Gator fans that a fire at Auburn's football dorm had destroyed 20 books: "But the real tragedy was that 15 hadn't been colored yet." (1991)

Jim Finks, New Orleans Saints G.M., when asked after a loss what he thought of the refs: "I'm not allowed to comment on lousy officiating." (1986)

Read This; It's Funny!!

Alan Kulwicki, stock car racer, on racing Saturday nights as opposed to Sunday afternoons: "It's basically the same, just darker."(1991)

Lincoln Kennedy, Oakland Raiders tackle, on his decision not to vote: "I was going to write myself in, but I was afraid I'd get shot."(1996)

Frank Layden, Utah Jazz president, on a former player: "I told him, 'Son, what is it with you. Is it ignorance or apathy?' He said, 'Coach, I don't know and I don't care.'" (1991)

Torrin Polk, University of Houston receiver, on his coach, John Jenkins: "He treats us like men. He lets us wear earrings." (1991)

Shelby Metcalf, basketball coach at Texas A&M, recounting what he told a player who received four F's and one D: "Son, looks to me like you're spending too much time on one subject." (1987)

Stories

Subject: My Class Reunion 214
Subject: Michael the Dragon Master 217
Subject: Email From Heaven 218
Subject: Bad Day 219
Subject: Moving to Arizona 220
Subject: Please Help 222
Subject: Snow 224
Subject: Rat Race Explained.... 227
Subject: Where's Ethyl? 228
Subject: Cigars 230

Read This; It's Funny!!

Subject: My Class Reunion

I had prepared for it like any intelligent woman would. I went on a starvation diet the day before, knowing that all the extra weight would just melt off in 24 hours, leaving me with my sleek, trim, high-school body.

The last many years of careful cellulite collection Would just be gone with a snap of the finger. I knew if I didn't eat a morsel on Friday, that I could probably fit into my senior formal on Saturday.

Trotting up to the attic, I pulled the gown out of the garment bag, carried it lovingly downstairs, ran my hand over the fabric, and hung it on the door. I stripped naked, looked in the mirror, sighed, and thought, "Well okay, maybe if I shift it all to the back..." bodies never have pockets where you need them. Bravely, I took the gown off the hanger, unzipped the shimmering dress and stepped gingerly into it. I struggled, twisted, turned, and pulled and I got the formal all the way up to my knees...before the zipper gave out.

I was disappointed. I wanted to wear that dress with those silver platform sandals again and dance the night away. Okay, one setback was not going to spoil my mood for this affair. No way! Rolling the dress into a ball and tossing it into the corner,

I turned to Plan B, the black velvet caftan. I gathered up all the goodies that I had purchased at the drug store; the scented shower gel; the body-building, and highlighting shampoo and conditioner, and the split-end killer and shine enhancer. Soon my hair would look like that girl's in the Pantene ads.

Then the makeup—the under eye "ain't no lines here" finishing cream, the all-day face-lifting gravity-fighting moisturizer with wrinkle filler spackle; the all day "kiss me till my lips bleed, and see if this gloss will come off" lipstick, the bronzing face powder for that special glow...But first, the roll-on facial hair remover. I could feel the wrinkles shuddering in fear.

OK - time to get ready... I jumped into the steaming shower, soaped, lathered, rinsed, shaved, and tweezed, buffed, scrubbed, and scoured my body to a tingling pink. I plastered my freshly scrubbed face with the anti-wrinkle, gravity fighting, "your face will look like a baby's butt" face cream. I set my hair on the hot rollers.

214

I felt wonderful. Ready to take on the world. Or in this instance, my underwear. With the towel firmly wrapped around my glistening body, I pulled out the black lace, tummy-tucking, cellulite-pushing, ham hock-rounding girdle, and the matching "lifting those bosoms like they're filled with helium" bra.

I greased my body with the scented body lotion and began the plunge.

I pulled, stretched, tugged, hiked, folded, tucked, twisted, shimmied, hopped, pushed, wiggled, snapped, shook, caterpillar crawled, and kicked.

Sweat poured off my forehead but I was done. And it didn't look bad. So I rested. A well deserved rest, too. The girdle was on my body.

Bounce a quarter off my behind? It was tighter than a trampoline. Can you say, "Rubber baby buggy bumper butt?" Okay so I had to take baby steps, and walk sideways, and I couldn't move from my butt cheeks to my knees, But I was firm!

Oh no...I had to go to the bathroom. And there wasn't a snap crotch.

From now on, undies gotta have a snap crotch. I was ready to rip it open and re-stitch the crotch with Velcro, but the pain factor from past experiments was still fresh in my mind. I quickly side stepped to the bathroom. An hour later, I had answered nature's call and repeated the struggle into the girdle.

I was ready for the bra. I remembered what the saleslady said to do.

I could see her glossed lips mouthing, "Do not fasten the bra in the front, and twist it around. Put the bra on the way it should be worn— straps over the shoulders. Then bend over and gently place both breasts inside the cups. "Easy if you have four hands. But, with confidence, I put my arms into the holsters, bent over and pulled the bra down... but the boobs weren't cooperating. I'd no sooner tuck one in a cup, and while placing the other, the first would slip out. I needed a strategy. I bounced up and down a few times, tried to dribble them in with short bunny hops, but that didn't work. So, while bent over, I began rocking gently back and forth on my heel and toes and I set 'em to swinging. Finally, on the fourth swing, pause, and lift, I captured the gliding glands.

Quickly fastening the back of the bra, I stood up for examination.

Read This; It's Funny!!

Back straight, slightly arched, I turned and faced the mirror, turning front, and then sideways. I smiled. Yes, Houston, we have lift up!

My breasts were high, firm and there was cleavage! I was happy until I tried to look down. I had a chin rest. And I couldn't see my feet. I still had to put on my panty hose, and shoes. Oh........why did I buy heels with buckles?

Then I had to pee again.

I put on my sweats, fixed myself a drink, ordered pizza, and skipped the reunion.

Subject: Michael the Dragon Master

Michael the Dragon Master was an official in King Arthur's court. He had a long-standing obsession to nuzzle the beautiful Queen's voluptuous breasts. But he knew the penalty for this would be death.

One day he revealed his secret desire to his colleague, Horatio, who was the King's chief physician. Horatio said, "I can arrange it, but I will need 1,000 gold coins to pay bribes". Michael the Dragon Master Readily agreed. The next day Horatio made up a batch of itching lotion and poured a little of it into the Queen's brassiere while she was taking a bath.

Soon after she dressed the itching commenced and grew in intensity.

Upon being called to the royal chambers, Horatio told the King that only a special saliva, if applied for four hours, would cure this type of itch, and that tests had shown such a saliva was only to be found in Michael the Dragon Master's mouth.

King Arthur summoned Michael the Dragon Master.

Michael the Dragon Master slipped the antidote to the itching lotion, which Horatio had given him, into his mouth and for the next four hours worked passionately on the Queen's magnificent breasts.

Satisfied, he returned to his chamber and found Horatio demanding payment.

However, with his obsession now satisfied, he refused to pay Horatio anything and shooed him away, knowing that Horatio could never report this matter to the King.

The next day, Horatio slipped a massive dose of the same itching Lotion onto King Arthur's loincloth. King Arthur summoned Michael the Dragon Master.....

Moral of the story: Pay your bills.

Read This; It's Funny!!

Subject: Email From Heaven

It seems there was this couple from Minneapolis, Minnesota who decided to go to Florida for a few days to thaw out during one particularly cold winter. Because both of them worked, they had some difficulty coordinating travel schedules. They finally decided that the husband would leave for Florida on a certain day and the wife would follow him the day after. The man made it down to Florida as planned and went directly to his hotel.

Once in his room, he decided to open his laptop and send his wife, who was still back in Minnesota, an e-mail. However, he accidentally left off one letter in typing his wife's e-mail address and sent the e-mail off without realizing his error.

In another part of the country a widow had just returned from the funeral of her husband, a Lutheran Pastor of many years, who had been "called home to glory" just a few days earlier. She decided to check her e-mail because she was expecting to hear from her husband's relatives and friends. Upon reading the first message she let out a loud scream, fainted and fell to the floor. The woman's son rushed into the room and found his mother lying on the floor.

He glanced up at the computer screen and saw the following:

To: My Loving Wife.

Subject: I've arrived!

I've just checked in. Everything has been prepared for your arrival here tomorrow. Looking forward to seeing you then!

Your Devoted Husband.

Subject: Bad Day

An insurance company asked for more information regarding a work related accident claim. This was the response:

I put poor planning as the cause for my accident. I am an amateur radio operator, and was working on the top section of my new 80 foot tower.

When I had completed my work, I discovered that I had brought up about 300 pounds of tools and spare hardware. Rather than carry the materials down by hand, I decided to lower the items using a pulley. Securing the rope at ground level, I went to the top of the tower and loaded the tools into a small barrel. Then I went back to the ground and untied the rope, holding it tightly to ensure a slow descent of the 300 pounds of tools. You will note in Block 11 of the accident report that I weigh 155 pounds.

Due to my surprise of being jerked off the ground so suddenly, I lost my presence of mind and forgot to let go of the rope. I proceeded at a rather rapid rate of speed up the side of the tower. In the vicinity of the 40 foot level, I met the barrel coming down. This explains my fractured skull and broken collarbone.

Slowed only slightly, I continued my rapid ascent, not stopping until the fingers of my right hand were two knuckles deep into the pulley.

I regained my presence of mind, and was able to hold onto the rope in spite of my pain. At the same time, however, the barrel of tools hit the ground and the bottom fell out of the barrel.. Devoid of the weight of the tools, the barrel now weighed approximately 20 pounds. I refer you again to my weight in Block 11.

As you might imagine, I began a rapid descent down the side of the tower. In the vicinity of the 40 foot level, I met the barrel coming up. This accounts for the two fractured ankles, and the lacerations on my legs and lower body.

The encounter with the barrel slowed me enough to lessen my injuries when I fell into the pile of tools, so only three vertebra were cracked.

I am sorry to report, however, that as I lay on the tools, in pain, unable to stand and watch the empty barrel 80 feet above me, I again lost my presence of mind, and let go of the rope....

After all this I can say I learned something to remember !

Read This; It's Funny!!

Subject: Moving to Arizona

May 30th
   Now this is a state that knows how to live!! Beautiful sunny days and warm balmy evenings. Mountains and deserts blended together. What a place!
   Watched the sunset from a park lying on a blanket. It was beautiful.
   I've finally found my home. I love it here.

June 14th
   Really heating up. Got to 100 today. Not a problem. Live in an air-conditioned home, drive an air-conditioned car. What a pleasure to see the sun every day like this. I'm turning into a real sun worshipper.

June 30th
   Had the backyard landscaped with western plants today. Lots of cactus and rocks. What a breeze to maintain. No more mowing for me. Another scorcher today, but I love it here.

July 10th
   The temperature hasn't been below 100 all week. How do people get used to this kind of heat? At least it's a dry heat. Getting used to it is taking longer than I expected.

July 15th
   Fell asleep by the pool. (Got 3rd degree burns over 60% of my body.) Missed two days of work, what a dumb thing to do. I learned my lesson though: got to respect the ol' sun in a climate like this.

July 20th
   I missed Tabby (our cat) sneaking into the car when I left this morning.
   By the time I got out to the hot car for lunch, Tabby had swollen up to the size of a shopping bag and exploded all over $2,000 worth of leather upholstery.
   I told the kids she ran away. The car now smells like Kibbles and sh*t.
   No more pets in this heat!

220

July 25th

Dry heat, my butt. Hot is hot!! The home air-conditioner is on the fritz and AC repairman charged $200 just to drive by and tell me he needed to order parts.

July 30th

Been sleeping outside by the pool for three nights now. $1,100 in dam* house payments and we can't even go inside. Why did I ever come here?

Aug 4th

115 degrees. Finally got the air-conditioner fixed today. It cost $500 and gets the temperature down to about 90. Stupid repairman peed in my pool. I hate this state.

Aug 8th

If another wise guy cracks, "Hot enough for you today?", I'm going to tear his throat out. Dam* heat. By the time I get to work the radiator is boiling over, my clothes are soaking wet, and I smell like roasted Garfield!!

Aug 10th

The weather report might as well be a freaking recording: Hot and Sunny.

It's been too hot to make love for two dam* months and the weatherman says it might really warm up next week. Doesn't it ever rain in this barren desert?? Water rationing has been in effect all summer, so $1,700 worth of cactus just dried up and blew into the pool. Even a cactus can't live in this heat!!

Aug 14th

Welcome to Hell!!! Temperature got to 123 today. Forgot to crack the window and blew the windshield out of the Lincoln. The installer came to fix it and said, "Hot enough for you today?" My wife had to spend the $1,100 house payment to bail me out of jail.

Aug 30th

Worst day of the summer. The monsoon rains finally came and all they did is to make it muggier than hell. The Lincoln is now floating somewhere in Mexico with it's new $500 windshield. That does it, we're moving to New York for some peace and quiet!

221

Read This; It's Funny!!

Subject: Please Help

I've never forwarded one of these before, but this one was different...it really touched me.

My name is Billy Evans. I am a very sick little boy. My mother is typing this for me, because I can't. She is crying. The reason she is so sad is because I'm so sick.

I was born without a body. It doesn't hurt, except when I try to breathe. The doctors gave me an artificial body. It is a burlap bag filled with leaves. The doctors said that was the best they could do on account of us having no money or insurance. I would like to have a body transplant, but we need more money. Mommy doesn't work because she said nobody hires crying people.

I said, "Don't cry, Mommy," and she hugged my burlap bag. Mommy always gives me hugs, even though she's allergic to burlap and it makes her sneeze and chafes her real bad.

I hope you will help me. You can help me if you forward this email to everyone you know. Forward it to people you don't know, too.

Dr. Johansen said that for every person you forward this email to, Bill Gates will team up with AOL and send a nickel to NASA. With that funding, NASA will collect prayers from school children all over America and have the astronauts take them up into space so that the angels can hear them better. Then they will come back to earth and go to the Pope, and he will take up a collection in church and send all the money to the doctors.

The doctors could help me get better then.

Maybe one day I will be able to play baseball. Right now I can only be third base.

Every time you forward this letter, the astronauts can take more prayers to the angels and my dream will be closer to coming true.

Please help me. Mommy is so sad, and I want a body. I don't want my leaves to rot before I turn 10.

If you don't forward this email, that's okay. Mommy says you're a mean and heartless bastard who doesn't care about a poor little boy with only a head. She says that if you don't stew in the raw pit of your own guilt-ridden stomach, she hopes you die a long slow, horrible death and then burn forever in hell. What kind of cruel person are you that you can't take five f***in' minutes to forward this to all your friends so that they can feel guilt and shame about ignoring a poor, bodiless nine-year-old?

Please help me. I try to be happy, but it's hard. I wish I had a kitty. I wish I could hold a kitty. I wish I could hold a kitty that wouldn't chew on me and try to bury its turds in the leaves of my burlap body. I wish that very much.

Thank You,
Billy "Smiles" Evans

Read This; It's Funny!!

Subject: Snow

December 8: 6:00 PM. It started to snow. The first snow of the season and the wife and I took our cocktails and sat for hours by the window watching the huge soft flakes drift down from heaven. It looked like a Grandma Moses Print. So romantic, we felt like newlyweds again. I love snow!

December 9: We woke to a beautiful blanket of crystal white snow covering every inch of the landscape. What a fantastic sight! Can there be a more lovely place in the Whole World? Moving here was the best idea I've ever had. Shoveled for the first time in years and felt like a boy again. I did both our driveway and the sidewalks. This afternoon the snowplow came along and covered up the sidewalks and closed in the driveway, so I got to shovel again. What a perfect life.

December 12: The sun has melted all our lovely snow. Such a disappointment. My neighbor tells me not to worry, we'll definitely have a white Christmas. No snow on Christmas would be awful! Bob says we'll have so much snow by the end of winter, that I'll never want to see snow again. I don't think that's possible. Bob is such a nice man I'm glad he's our neighbor.

December 14: Snow lovely snow! 8" last night. The temperature dropped to -20. The cold makes everything sparkle so. The wind took my breath away, but I warmed up by shoveling the driveway and sidewalks. This is the life! The snowplow came back this afternoon and buried everything again. I didn't realize I would have to do quite this much shoveling, but I'll certainly get back in shape this way. I wish I wouldn't huff and puff so.

December 15: 20 inches forecast. Sold my van and bought a 4x4 Blazer. Bought snow tires for the wife's car and 2 extra shovels. Stocked the freezer. The wife wants a wood stove in case the electricity goes out. I think that's silly. We aren't in Alaska, after all.

December 16: Ice storm this morning. Fell on my hind end on the ice in the driveway putting down salt. Hurt like crazy. The wife laughed for an hour, which I think was very cruel.

224

December 17: Still way below freezing. Roads are too icy to go anywhere. Electricity was off for 5 hours. I had to pile the blankets on to stay warm. Nothing to do but stare at the wife and try not to irritate her. Guess I should've bought a wood stove, but won't admit it to her. Man, I hate it when she's right. I can't believe I'm freezing to death in my own living room.

December 20: Electricity's back on, but had another 14" of the stuff last night. More shoveling. Took all day. The snowplow came by twice. Tried to find a neighbor kid to shovel, but they said they're too busy playing hockey. I think they're lying. Called the only hardware store around to see about buying a snow blower and they're out. Might have another shipment in March. I think they're lying. Bob says I have to shovel or the city will have it done and bill me. I think he's lying.

December 22: Bob was right about a white Christmas because 13 more inches of the white crud fell today and it's so cold it probably won't melt till August. Took me 45 minutes to get all dressed up to go out to shovel and then I had to go to the bathroom. By the time I got undressed, used the bathroom and dressed again, I was too tired to shovel. Tried to hire Bob who has a plow on his truck for the rest of the winter; but he says he's too busy. I think the jerk is lying.

December 23: Only 2" of snow today. And it warmed up to 0. The wife wanted me to decorate the front of the house this morning. What! Is she nuts??? Why didn't she tell me to do that a month ago? She says she did but I think she's lying.

December 24: 6". Snow packed so hard by snowplow, l broke the shovel. Thought I was having a heart attack. If I ever catch the jerk who drives that snowplow, I'll drag him through the snow by his ears. I know he hides around the corner and waits for me to finish shoveling and then he comes down the street at a 100 miles an hour and throws snow all over where I've just been! Tonight the wife wanted me to sing Christmas carols with her and open our presents, but I was busy watching for the stupid snowplow.

Read This; It's Funny!!

December 25: Merry Christmas. 20 more inches of the slop tonight. Snowed in. The idea of shoveling makes my blood boil. Man I hate the snow! Then the snowplow driver came by asking for a donation and I hit him over the head with my shovel. The wife says I have a bad attitude. I think she's an idiot. If I have to watch "It's a Wonderful Life" one more time, I'm going to choke her.

December 26: Still snowed in. Why did I ever move here? It was all HER idea. She's really getting on my nerves.

December 27: Temperature dropped to -50 and the pipes froze, but at least it is too cold to snow!!!!!!!!

December 28: Warmed up to above -30, still can't snow any more though. Still snowed in and THE WIFE is driving me crazy!!!

December 29: 10 more inches. Bob says I have to shovel the roof or it could cave in. That's the silliest thing I ever heard. How dumb does he think I am?

December 30: Roof caved in. The snow plow driver is suing me for a million dollars for the bump on his head. The wife went home to her mother. 9" predicted.

December 31: Set fire to what's left of the house. No more shoveling.

January 8: I feel so good. I just love those little white pills they keep giving me. Why am I tied to the bed?

Subject: Rat Race Explained....

A boat docked in a tiny Mexican village. An American tourist complimented the Mexican fisherman on the quality of his fish and asked how long it took him to catch them.

"Not very long," answered the Mexican.

"Well, then, why didn't you stay out longer and catch more?" asked the American.

The Mexican explained that his small catch was sufficient to meet his needs and those of his family.

The American asked, "But what do you do with the rest of your time?"

"I sleep late, fish a little, play with my children, and take a siesta with my wife. In the evenings, I go into the village to see my friends, have a few drinks, play the guitar, and sing a few songs...I have a full life."

The American interrupted, "I have an MBA from Harvard and I can help you! You should start by fishing longer every day. You can then sell the extra fish you catch. With the extra revenue, you can buy a bigger boat. With the extra money the larger boat will bring, you can buy a second one and a third one and so on until you have an entire fleet of trawlers. Instead of selling your fish to a middle man, you can negotiate directly with the processing plants and maybe even open your own plant. You can then leave this little village and move to Mexico City, Los Angeles, or even New York City! From there you can direct your huge enterprise."

"How long would that take?" asked the Mexican.

"Twenty, perhaps twenty-five years," replied the American.

"And after that?"

"Afterwards? That's when it gets really interesting," answered the American, laughing. "When your business gets really big, you can start selling stocks and make millions!"

"Millions? Really? And after that?"

"After that you'll be able to retire, live in a tiny village near the coast, sleep late, play with your children, catch a few fish, take siestas with your wife, and spend your evenings drinking and enjoying your friends."

Read This; It's Funny!!

Subject: Where's Ethyl?

Sometimes I really get upset with my husband for not giving me credit for being as smart as I am. Just like the other morning when I rode to his office with him so I could have the car. As we drove by a service station, he turned to glance back.

"Well, I see another business is getting rid of their Ethyl," he remarked.

"Ethyl who?" I asked curiously.

"Ethyl Gas," he said in an annoyed tone.

"What a terrible name," I said. "If I had one like that, I'd change it. Why are they getting rid of Ethyl, do you suppose?"

"Well, since everything's gotten so high, people just can't afford Ethyl anymore," he answered.

"Just what line of work is Ethyl in, anyway?" I inquired.

"You KNOW what Ethyl is," he snapped. " There's regular and then there's Ethyl."

"I don't like the way you said that," I frowned, "You say it like you would, 'There's Lily Tomlin and then there's Dolly Parton.' Which class would I fit in?"

"Good grief," he exclaimed, "you're not either one."

"Thanks a lot, I guess I know where that leaves me."

"Look," he said, growing more exasperated, "Are you a fuel?"

"I certainly am not," I growled, "unless you know something I don't - and I'm beginning to wonder. You sure know a lot about Ethyl."

"Let's just drop the subject," he muttered. "But be sure and remind me when I get out to tell Bill about this."

"Why?" I asked.

"Because he usually stops there on his way home to get Ethyl." he replied.

"You're kidding!" I exclaimed. " And he's got three kids. Does his wife know he stops there to get Ethyl?"

"Well, sure," my husband answered. "She stops with him a lot of times."

"Do you mean to tell me he stops and gets Ethyl when his wife is right there with him?"

"He sure does - in fact, I saw his wife put Ethyl in the car one time."

"I can't believe that." I yelled. "She must be nuts about him - she'll put up with anything. Let me ask you something," I said seriously. "Have YOU ever stopped there to get Ethyl?"

"You know I've never put Ethyl in this car," he grumbled. "This car wouldn't run right with Ethyl in it."

"You better believe it," I said. "In fact, if you put Ethyl in this car, it would never run again after I got through with it."

"Do me a favor," he said, as he stopped the car to get out. "Don't tell anyone about this conversation. No one would believe my wife is so naive she doesn't know about Ethyl."

Well, I've got news for him. I'm not half as naive as he thinks I am. I found out where Ethyl went. I just happened to drive by a place the other day that had a big sign out in front proclaiming proudly, "WE HAVE ETHYL."

And I've been watching that place ever since.

Read This; It's Funny!!

Subject: Cigars

A Charlotte, NC, lawyer purchased a box of very rare and expensive cigars, then insured them against fire among other things. Within a month having smoked his entire stockpile of these great cigars and without yet having made even his first premium payment on the policy, the lawyer filed a claim against the insurance company. In his claim, the lawyer stated the cigars were lost "in a series of small fires." The insurance company refused to pay, citing the obvious reason: that the man had consumed the cigars in the normal fashion.

The lawyer sued....and won! In delivering the ruling the judge agreed with the insurance company that the claim was frivolous. The Judge stated nevertheless, that the lawyer held a policy from the company in which it had warranted that the cigars were insurable and also guaranteed that it would insure them against fire, without defining what is considered to be "unacceptable fire," and was obligated to pay the claim.

Rather than endure a lengthy and costly appeal process, the insurance company accepted the ruling and paid $15,000.00 to the lawyer for his loss of the rare cigars lost in the "fires."

NOW FOR THE BEST PART... After the lawyer cashed the check, the insurance company had him arrested on 24 counts of ARSON!!!! With his own insurance claim and testimony from the previous case being used against him, the lawyer was convicted of intentionally burning his insured property and was sentenced to 24 months in jail and a $24,000.00 fine.

This is a true story and was the 1st place winner in the recent Criminal Lawyers Award Contest.

The South

Subject: Movin to Texas? 232
Subject: Redneck Etiquette 235
Subject: Redneck Valentines Day Poem 237
Subject: Southern Advice 240
Subject: Southern Expressions 242
Subject: Girls Raised in the South 243
Subject: Southern Knowledge 246
Subject: Texas First Aid..248
Subject: You Know You're a Texan When 249
Subject: You Might be a Redneck Jedi if..... 251
Subject: It's a Texas Thing.. 252

Read This; It's Funny!!

Subject: Movin to Texas?

1. Save all manner of bacon grease. You will be instructed later how to use it.
2. Just because you can drive on snow and ice does not mean we can. Stay home the two days of the year it snows.
3. If you do run your car into a ditch, don't panic. Four men in the cab of a four wheel drive with a 12-pack of beer and a tow chain will be along shortly. Don't try to help them. Just stay out of their way. This is what they live for.
4. Don't be surprised to find movie rentals and bait in the same store.
5. Remember: "Y'all" is singular."All y'all" is plural. "All y'all's" is plural possessive.
6. Get used to hearing, "You ain't from around here, are you?"
7. If you are yelling at the person driving 15 mph in a 55 mph zone, directly in the middle of the road, remember, many folks learned to drive on a model of vehicle known as John Deere, and this is the proper speed and lane position for that vehicle.
8. If you hear a redneck exclaim, "Hey, y'all, watch this!" Stay out of his way. These are likely the last words he will ever say.
9. Get used to the phrase, "It's not the heat. It's the humidity." And the collateral phrase, "You call this hot? Wait'll August."
10. There are no delis. Don't ask.
11. In conversation, never put your hand on a man's shoulder when making a point, especially in a bar.
12. Chili does NOT have beans in it.
13. Brisket is not 'cooked' in an oven.
14. Don't tell us how you did it up there. Nobody cares.
15. If you think it's too hot, don't worry. It'll cool down in December.
16. We do TOO have 4 seasons: December, January, February, and Summer!
17. A Mercedes-Benz is not a status symbol. A Ford-150 is.
18. If someone tells you, "Don't worry, those peppers aren't hot," you can be certain they are.
19. If you fail to heed my warning in # 18 above, be sure to have a bowl of guacamole handy. Water won't do.
20. Rocky Mountain oysters are NOT oysters. Don't ask.
21. If someone says they're "fixin" to do something, that doesn't mean anything's broken.
22. "Tea" = Iced tea. There is no other kind.

23. If you don't understand our passion for college and high school football, just keep your mouth shut.

24. The value of a parking space is not determined by the distance to the door, but the availability of shade.

25. If someone wants to pass you on a two lane road, pull onto the shoulder, that is called "courtesy".

26. BBQ is a food group. It does NOT mean grilling burgers and hot dogs outdoors.

26. No matter what you've seen on TV, line dancing is not a popular weekend pastime.

28. Everything goes better with Ranch dressing.

29. Don't wear a hat of any kind indoors. Ever!

30. Women, stock up on your makeup. You look pale in Texas without 4 times what you're used to wearing.

31. And you'll need bigger hair, too.

32. Men, remove your earrings. Women, get some bigger ones.

33. Start thinking up names now for the bugs that will be living in your home with you. They will be plentiful and large. Raid won't kill them. They are the Native Texans, and you must co-exist in their home with them.

34. Stop saying "beer" and start saying "coldbeer." It's one word.

35. Men, do not ever, ever wear a Speedo to a swimming hole, pool, beach, or lake.

36. Leave your little yippy dog with your parents. You'll need a cow dog in Texas.

37. Don't speak about Tom Landry, ZZ Top, Stevie Ray Vaughan, or Earl Campbell without expressing your love and admiration.

38. Do not expect to find public land that you can hike, hunt, or fish on. There is a national park here and there, but mostly, our land is privately owned. Don't trespass! You knuckleheads use your state income taxes to buy up land. We don't have a state income tax, and we run cattle on our land.

39. Do not buy a house or car without air conditioning. You won't need a heater.

40. Learn to say "yes sir" and "yes ma'am" to anyone older than you.

41. Peel that "Gore 2000" bumper sticker off your car.

42. We really mean "Don't mess with Texas." That means don't litter.

43. If you're from New York, learn to say "Houston."

44. Don't talk about a rivalry between your home state and Texas. We are not aware of any competition.

45. Do not believe everything we say. We embellish. It's our job.
46. You'll need a car. We don't walk to the end of our driveways, and there is no mass transit. We don't share our roads with bicyclists either.
47. Our cops are not jerks, and they don't take bribes. Be polite.
48. You'll want to learn what the following critters look like a scorpion, tarantula, centipede, armadillo, javelina, and a horned toad. Only one of them will hurt you, but all of them will scare you badly. Brush up on your poisonous snakes, too. We've got 5 different kinds.
49. Anything carbonate is Coke. Coke is a generic term that can include anything from Sprite to Root Beer. And we don't drink Coke, we drink Dr. Pepper. Or tea.
50. YOU have the accent.

Subject: Redneck Etiquette

DRIVING ETIQUETTE
*Dim your headlights for approaching vehicles, even if the gun is loaded and the deer is in sight.
*When approaching a four-way stop, the vehicle with the largest tires always has the right of way.
*Never tow another car using pantyhose and duct tape.
*When sending your wife down the road with a gas can, it is impolite to ask her to bring back beer.
*Never relieve yourself from a moving vehicle, especially when driving.
*Do not remove the seats from the car so that all your kids can fit in.
*Do not lay rubber while traveling in a funeral procession.

PERSONAL HYGIENE
*Unlike clothes and shoes, a toothbrush should never be a hand-me-down item.
*If you have to vacuum the bed, it's time to change the sheets.
*While ears need to be cleaned regularly, this is a job that should be done in private using one's OWN truck keys.
*Plucking unwanted nose hair is time- consuming work. A cigarette lighter and a small tolerance for pain can accomplish the same goal and save hours.
Note: Its a good idea to keep a bucket of water handy when using this method.

DINING OUT
*Remember to leave a generous tip for good service. After all, their mobile home costs just as much as yours.

ENTERTAINING IN YOUR HOME
*A centerpiece for the table should never be anything prepared by a taxidermist.
*Do not allow the dog to eat at the table . . . no matter how good his manners are.
*If your dog falls in love with a guest's leg, have the decency to leave them alone for a few minutes.

Read This; It's Funny!!

DATING (Outside the Family)
*Always offer to bait your date's hook, especially on the first date.
*Be aggressive. Let her know you are interested: "I've been wanting to go out with you since I read that stuff on the men's bathroom wall two years a go."
*If a girl's name does not appear regularly on a bathroom wall, water tower, or an overpass, odds are good that the date will end in frustration.

THEATER ETIQUETTE
*Crying babies should be taken to the lobby and picked up immediately after the movie has ended.
*Refrain from talking to characters on the screen. Tests have proven they can't hear you.

WEDDINGS
*Livestock is usually a poor choice for a wedding gift.
*It is not okay for the groom to bring a date to a wedding.
*When dancing, never remove undergarments, no matter how hot it is.
*A bridal veil made of window screen is not only cost effective but also a proven fly deterrent.
*For the groom, at least rent a tux. A leisure suit with a cummerbund and a clean bowling shirt can create a natty appearance. Though uncomfortable, say yes to socks and shoes for this special occasion.

TIPS FOR ALL OCCASIONS
*Never take a beer to a job interview or ask if they press charges.
*Always identify people in your yard before shooting at them.
*Always say "Excuse me" after getting sick in someone else's car.
*It's considered tacky to take a cooler to church.
*Even if you're certain that you are included in the will, it's considered tacky to drive a U-Haul to the funeral home.
*The socially refined never fish coins out of public toilets, especially if other people are around.
*Always provide an alibi to the police for family members.

236

Subject: Redneck Valentines Day Poem

Straight from L.A. (Lower Alabama)

Collards is green,
my dog's name is Blue
and I'm so lucky
to have a sweet thang like you.

Yore hair is like cornsilk
a-flapping in the breeze.
Softer than Blue's
and without all them fleas.

You move like the bass,
which excite me in May.
You ain't got no scales
but I luv you anyway.

Yo're as satisfy'n as okry
jist a-fry'n in the pan.
Yo're as fragrant as "snuff"
right out of the can.

You have some'a yore teeth,
for which I am proud;
I hold my head high
when we're in a crowd.

On special occasions,
when you shave under yore arms,
well, I'm in hawg heaven,
and awed by yore charms.

Still them fellers at work,
they all want to know,
what I did to deserve
such a purdy, young doe.

Read This; It's Funny!!

Like a good roll of duct tape
yo're there fer yore man,
to patch up life's troubles
and fix what you can.

Yo're as cute as a junebug
 a-buzzin' overhead.
You ain't mean like those far ants
I found in my bed.

Cut from the best cloth
like a plaid flannel shirt,
you spark up my life
more than a fresh load of dirt.

When you hold me real tight
like a padded gunrack,
my life is complete;
Ain't nuttin' I lack.

Yore complexion, it's perfection,
like the best vinyl sidin'.
despite all the years,
yore age, it keeps hidin'.

Me 'n' you's like a Moon Pie
with a RC cold drank,
we go together
like a skunk goes with stank.

Some men, they buy chocolate
for Valentine's Day;
They git it at Wal-Mart,
it's romantic that way.

Some men git roses
on that special day
from the cooler at Kroger.
"That's impressive," I say.

Some men buy fine diamonds
from a flea market booth.
"Diamonds are forever,"
they explain, suave and couth.

But for this man,
honey, these won't do.
Cause yor'e too special,
you sweet thang you.

I got you a gift,
without taste nor odor,
more useful than diamonds...
IT'S A NEW TROLL'N MOTOR!!

Luv, from yor romeo

Read This; It's Funny!!

Subject: Southern Advice

If you are from the northern states and planning on visiting or moving to the South, there are a few things you should know that will help you adapt to the difference in lifestyles:

The North has coffee houses,
The South has Waffle Houses.

The North has dating services,
The South has family reunions.

The North has switchblade knives,
The South has Lee Press-on Nails.

The North has double last names,
The South has double first names.

The North has Ted Kennedy,
The South has Jesse Helms.

The North has Indy car races,
The South has stock car races.

The North has Cream of Wheat,
The South has grits.

The North has green salads,
The South has collard greens.

The North has lobsters,
The South has crawdads.

The North has the rust belt,
The South has the Bible Belt.

The North has sun-dried toe-mah-toes,
The South has 'mater samiches.

The North has an ambulance,
The South has an amalance.

The first Southern expression to creep into a transplanted Northerner's vocabulary is the adjective 'big ol' truck or 'big ol' boy. Most Northerners begin their Southern-influenced dialect this way. All of them are in denial about it.

If there is the prediction of the slightest chance of even the smallest accumulation of snow, your presence is required at the local grocery store. It doesn't matter whether you need anything or not. You just have to go there.

Do not be surprised to find that 10-year-olds own their own shotguns, they are proficient marksmen, and their Mammas taught them how to aim.

You may hear a Southerner say "Ought!" to a dog or child. This is short for "Y'all ought not do that!" and is the equivalent of saying "No!"

Don't be worried at not understanding what people are saying. They can't understand you either.

The proper pronunciation you learned in school is no longer proper.

Be advised that "He needed killin" is a valid defense here.

In the South, we have found that the best way to grow a lush green lawn is to pour gravel on it and call it a driveway.

AND REMEMBER:

If you do settle in the South and bear children, don't think we will accept them as Southerners. After all, if the cat had kittens in the oven, we wouldn't call 'em biscuits.

Have a good day! Send this to four people that ain't related to you, and I reckon your life will turn into a country music song fore you know it.

Read This; It's Funny!!

Subject: Southern Expressions

1. "Well, butter my butt and call me a biscuit."

2. "It's been hotter'n a goat's butt in a pepper patch."

3. "She fell out of the ugly tree and hit every branch on the way down."

4. "Have a cup of coffee, it's already been 'saucered and blowed.'"

5. "She's so stuck up, she'd drown in a rainstorm."

6. "It's so dry, the trees are bribing the dogs."

7. "My cow died last night so I don't need your bull."

8. "Don't pee down my back and tell me it's raining."

9. "He's as country as cornflakes."

10. "This is gooder'n s**t."

11. "Busier than a cat covering s**t on a marble floor."

12. "If things get any better, I may have to hire someone to help me enjoy it."

Subject: Girls Raised in the South

Southern girls know bad manners when they see them:
Drinking straight out of a can.
Not sending thank you notes.
Velvet after February.
White shoes before Easter or after Labor Day.

Southern girls appreciate their natural assets:
Dewy skin.
A winning smile.
That unforgettable, Southern drawl.

Southern girls know their manners:
"Yes, ma'am."
"Yes, sir."

Southern girls have a distinct way with fond expressions:
"Y'all come back!"
"Well, bless your heart."
"Drop by when you can."
"How's your mother?"
"Love your hair."

Southern girls don't sweat....they glisten.

Southern girls know their summer weather report:
Humidity
Humidity
Humidity

Southern girls know their three R's:
Rich
Richer
Richest

Southern girls know their vacation spots:
The Beach
The Beach
The Beach

Read This; It's Funny!!

Southern girls know the joys of June, July, and August:
Summer tans
Wide brimmed hats

Southern girls know everybody's first name:
Honey
Darlin'
Sugah

Southern girls know the movies that speak to their hearts:
Gone With the Wind
Fried Green Tomatoes
Driving Miss Daisy
Steel Magnolias

Southern girls know their religions:
Baptist
Methodist
Football

Southern girls know their country breakfasts:
Red-eye gravy
GRITS
Country ham
Mouth-watering homemade biscuits

Southern girls know their cities dripping with Southern charm:
Richmond
Charleston
Savannah
Birmingham
Nawlins'

Southern girls know their elegant gentlemen:
Men in uniform.
Men in tuxedos.
Rhett Butler, of course.

Y'all know Southern girls are quick on the drawl.

Southern girls know their prime real estate:
The Mall
The Beauty Salon

Southern girls know the three deadly sins:
Bad hair
Bad manners
Bad blind dates

Southern girls know men may come and go, but friends are fo'evah!

Now you run along, Sugah, and send this to some other Girls Raised In The South, i.e., Southern Belles. Or to some of your Yankee Girlfriends to make them green with envy!

Read This; It's Funny!!

Subject: Southern Knowledge

The Ten Commandments of Grits
1. Thou shalt not put syrup on thy Grits.
2. Thou shalt not eat Cream of Wheat and call it Grits; for this is blasphemy.
3. Thou shalt not covet thy neighbors Grits.
4. Thou shalt only use Salt, Butter and Cheese as toppings for thy Grits.
5. Thou shalt not eat Instant Grits.
6. Thou shalt not put syrup on thy Grits.
7. Thou shalt not put syrup on thy Grits.
8. Thou shalt not put syrup on thy Grits.
9. Thou shalt not put sugar on thy Grits either.
10. Thou shalt not put sugar or syrup on thy Grits.

Things a southerner wouldn't say:
We don't keep firearms in this house.
Has anybody seen the sideburn trimmer?
You can't feed that to the dog.
I thought Graceland was tacky.
No kids in the back of the pick-up, it's not safe.
Wrasslin's fake.
Honey, did you mail that donation to Greenpeace?
We're vegetarians.
Do you think my hair is too big?
I'll have grapefruit instead of biscuits and gravy.
Honey, these bonsai trees need watering?
Who's Richard Petty?
Give me the small bag of pork rinds.
Deer heads detract from the decor.
Spitting is such a nasty habit.
I just couldn't find a thing at Wal-Mart today.
Trim the fat off that steak.
Cappuccino tastes better than espresso.
The tires on that truck are too big.
I'll have the arugula and radicchio salad.
I've got it all on a floppy disk.
Unsweetened tea tastes better.
Would you like your fish poached or broiled?
My fiancee, Paula Jo, is registered at Tiffany's.
I've got two cases of Zima for the Super Bowl.

Little Debbie snack cakes have too many fat grams.
Checkmate.
She's too old to be wearing that bikini.
Does the salad bar have bean sprouts?
Hey, here's an episode of "Hee Haw" that we haven't seen.
I don't have a favorite college team.
I believe you cooked those green beans too long.
Those shorts ought to be a little longer, Darla.
Elvis who?
Be sure to bring my salad dressing on the side.

Read This; It's Funny!!

Subject: Texas First Aid

Two Texans were having the blue plate special at their favorite watering hole, when they heard this awful choking sound. They turned around to see a lady, a few bar stools down, turning blue from wolfing down an Armadillo Burger too fast.

The first Texan said to the other, "Think we otta' help?"

"Yep," said the second Texan.

The first Texan got up and walked over to the lady and asked, "Kin yew breathe?"

She frantically shook her head no.

"Kin you speak?" he asked.

Again she frantically shook her head no.

With that, he helped her to her feet, lifted up her skirt, and began to lick her butt. She was so shocked, she coughed up the obstructing food and began to breathe with great relief.

The Texan then turned back to his friend and said, "Funny how that there Hind Lick Maneuver works every time!"

Subject: You Know You're a Texan When

You no longer associate bridges (or rivers) with water...
You can say 110 degrees without fainting...
You eat hot chilis to cool your mouth off...
You can make 'instant' sun tea...
You learn that a seat belt makes a pretty good branding iron...
The temperature drops below 95, and you feel a bit chilly...
You discover that in July, it takes only 2 fingers to drive your truck.
   (not only July....May through October!)
You discover that you can get a sunburn through your truck window...
Hot water now comes out of both taps...
It's noon in July, kids are on summer vacation, and not one person is out on the streets...
You actually burn your hand opening the truck door...
You break a sweat the instant you step outside..at 7:30, before work...
No one would dream of putting vinyl upholstery in a truck, or not having air conditioning...
Your biggest bicycle wreck fear is, "What if I get knocked out and end up lying on the pavement and cook to death...
You realize that asphalt has a liquid state...

It's so hot in Texas:

The birds have to use pot holders to pull worms out of the ground...
The potatoes cook underground and all you have to do to have lunch is to pull one out, and add butter, salt and pepper...
Farmers are feeding their chickens crushed ice to keep them from laying hard-boiled eggs...

It's so dry in Texas:
   The cows are giving evaporated milk...
   The trees are whistlin' for the dogs...

A sad Texan once prayed:
   "I wish it would rain - not so much for me, cuz I've seen it - but for my 7-year old, who hasn't...

Read This; It's Funny!!

A visitor to Texas once asked, "Does it ever rain out here?"

A rancher quickly answered, "Yes, it does. Do you remember that part in the Bible where it rained 40 days and 40 nights?" The visitor replied, "Yes, I'm familiar with Noah's flood"

"Well," the rancher puffed up, "we got about two and a half inches during that spell."

Subject: You Might be a Redneck Jedi if.....

You ever heard the phrase, "May the force be with y'all."

Your Jedi robe is camouflage.

You have ever used your light saber to open a bottle of Bud Light.

At least one wing of your X-Wings is primer colored.

You can easily describe the taste of an Ewok.

You have ever had a land-speeder up on blocks in your yard.

The worst part of spending time on Dagobah is the dadgum skeeters.

Wookies are offended by your B.O.

You have ever used the force to get yourself another beer so you didn't have to wait for a commercial.

You have ever used the force in conjunction with fishing/bowling.

Your father has ever said to you, "Shoot, son come on over to the dark side...it'll be a hoot."

You have ever had your R-2 unit use its self-defense electro-shock thingy to get the barbecue grill to light.

You have a confederate flag painted on the hood of your land-speeder.

You ever fantasized about Princess Leah wearing Daisy Duke shorts.

You have the doors of your X-wing welded shut and you have to get in through the window.

Although you had to kill him, you kinda thought that Jabba the Hutt had a pretty good handle on how to treat his women.

You have a cousin who bears a strong resemblance to Chewbacca.

You suggested that they outfit the Millennium Falcon with redwood deck.

You were the only person drinking Jack Daniels during the cantina scene.

You have bantha horns on the front of your landspeeder.

You describe the taste of an Ewok as "jus' like chicken."

You have ever used the force to get yourself another beer so you wouldn't have to wait for a commercial.

You have ever accidentally referred to Darth Vader's evil empire "them dam Yankees."

In your opinion, that Cee-Threepio fellow "just ain't right."

The REAL reason you got into a fight in the cantina was because you ordered Bud Light...and they didn't have it.

If you hear . . . "Luke, I am your father...and your uncle."

Read This; It's Funny!!

Subject: It's a Texas Thing..

ARE YOU FROM TEXAS?
YOU KNOW YOU'RE FROM TEXAS IF:
1. You measure distance in minutes.
2. You've ever had to switch from "heat" to "A/C" in the same day.
3. Stores don't have bags; they have sacks.
4. Stores don't have shopping carts; they have buggies.
5. You see a car running in the parking lot at the store with no one in it no matter what time of the year.
6. You use "fix" as a verb. Example: I am fixing to go to the store.
7. All the festivals across the state are named after a fruit, vegetable, grain, or animal.
8. You install security lights on your house and garage and leave both doors unlocked.
9. You carry jumper cables in your car ... for your OWN car.
10. You only own four spices: salt, pepper, ketchup, and Tabasco.
11. You think everyone from a bigger city has an accent.
12. You think sexy lingerie is a tee shirt and boxer shorts.
13. The local paper covers national and international news on one page but requires 6 pages for sports.
14. You think that the first day of deer season is a national holiday.
15. You know which leaves make good toilet paper.
16. You find 90 degrees F "a little warm."
17. You know all four seasons: Almost Summer, Summer, Still Summer, and Christmas.
18. You know whether another Texan is from southern, middle, or northern Texas as soon as they open their mouth.
19. There is a Dairy Queen in every town with a population of 1000 or more.
20. Going to Wal-Mart is a favorite past-time known as "goin wal-martin" or off to "Wally World."
21. You describe the first cool snap (below 70 degrees) as good chili weather.
22. You understand these jokes and forward them to your friends from Texas.

Words of Wisdom

Subject: Brilliant...... 254
Subject: Great Truths For Adults 257
Subject: Zen 258

Read This; It's Funny!!

Subject: Brilliant

You'll feel brilliant after you read these quotes...I did

Question: If you could live forever, would you and why? Answer:
"I would not live forever, because we should not live forever,
because if we were supposed to live forever, then we would live
forever, but we cannot live forever, which is why I would not
live forever,"
—Miss Alabama in the 1994 Miss USA contest.

"Whenever I watch TV and see those poor starving kids all over
the world, I can't help but cry. I mean I'd love to be skinny like
that, but not with all those flies and death and stuff,"
—Mariah Carey

"Smoking kills. If you're killed, you've lost a very important part
of your life,"
—Brooke Shields, during an interview to become spokesperson
for federal anti-smoking campaign.

"I've never had major knee surgery on any other part of my
body,"
—Winston Bennett, University of Kentucky basketball forward.

"Outside of the killings, Washington has one of the lowest crime
rates in the country,"
—Mayor Marion Barry, Washington, DC.

"I'm not going to have some reporters pawing through our papers.
We are the president,"
—Hillary Clinton commenting on the release of subpoenaed
documents.

"That lowdown scoundrel deserves to be kicked to death by a
jackass, and I'm just the one to do it,"
—A congressional candidate in Texas.

"We don't necessarily discriminate. We simply exclude certain
types of people."
—Colonel Gerald Wellman, ROTC Instructor.

"I don't feel we did wrong in taking this great country away from them. There were great numbers of people who needed new land, and the Indians were selfishly trying to keep it for themselves."
—John Wayne

"Half this game is ninety percent mental."
—Philadelphia Phillies manager, Danny Ozark

"It isn't pollution that's harming the environment. It's the impurities in our air and water that are doing it."
—Al Gore, Vice President

"I love California. I practically grew up in Phoenix."
—Dan Quayle

"It's no exaggeration to say that the undecideds could go one way or another."
—George Bush, US President

"We've got to pause and ask ourselves: How much clean air do we need?"
—Lee Iacocca

"I was provided with additional input that was radically different from the truth. I assisted in furthering that version."
—Colonel Oliver North, from his Iran-Contra testimony.

"If we don't succeed, we run the risk of failure."
—Bill Clinton, President

"We are ready for an unforeseen event that may or may not occur."
—Al Gore, VP

"Traditionally, most of Australia's imports come from overseas."
—Keppel Enderbery

"Your food stamps will be stopped effective March 1992 because we received notice that you passed away.
May God bless you. You may reapply if there is a change in your circumstances."

Read This; It's Funny!!

—Department of Social Services, Greenville, South Carolina

"If somebody has a bad heart, they can plug this jack in at night as they go to bed and it will monitor their heart throughout the night.
And the next morning, when they wake up dead, there'll be a record."
—Mark S. Fowler, FCC Chairman

...Feeling brilliant yet?
Send it on to your other genius friends, like I am doing.

Subject: Great Truths For Adults

Raising teenagers is like nailing Jell-O to a tree.

There is always a lot to be thankful for if you take time to look for it. For example, I am sitting here thinking how nice it is that wrinkles don't hurt.

You know you're getting old when you stoop to tie your shoes and wonder what else you can do while you're down there.

Reason to smile: Every seven minutes of every day, someone in an aerobics class pulls a hamstring.

The best way to keep kids at home is to make the home a pleasant atmosphere ... and let the air out of their tires.

Car sickness is the feeling you get when the monthly car payment is due.

Families are like fudge .. mostly sweet with a few nuts.

Today's mighty oak is just yesterday's nut that held its ground.

Laughing helps. It's like jogging on the inside.

Middle age is when you choose your cereal for the fiber, not the toy.

My mind not only wanders, sometimes it leaves completely.

The more you complain, the longer God lets you live.

One day I shall burst my buds of calm and blossom into hysteria.

If you can remain calm, you just don't have all the facts.

Life's golden age is when the kids are too old to need baby sitters and too young to borrow the family car.

Read This; It's Funny!!

Subject: Zen

Your Daily Moment of Zen
(Modified to reflect contemporary wisdom):

1. Do not walk behind me, for I may not lead. Do not walk ahead of me, for I may not follow. Do not walk beside me either. Just leave me the hell alone.

2. It's always darkest before dawn. So if you're going to steal your neighbor's newspaper, that's the time to do it.

3. Sex is like air. It's not important unless you aren't getting any.

4. Don't be irreplaceable. If you can't be replaced, you can't be promoted.

5. No one is listening until you fart.

6. Always remember you're unique. Just like everyone else.

7. If at first you don't succeed, skydiving is not for you.

8. If you tell the truth, you don't have to remember anything.

9. Don't worry; it only seems kinky the first time.

10. Duct tape is like the Force. It has a light side and a dark side, and it holds the universe together.

11. Generally speaking, you aren't learning much when your lips are moving.

12. Experience is something you don't get until just after you need it.

13. We are born naked, wet, and hungry, and get slapped on our ass ... then things get worse .

14. Eat a live toad first thing in the morning, and nothing worse can happen to you the rest of the day!

Words of Wisdom

The most wasted day of all is one in which we have not laughed.

History

Subject: Class of 2002 261
Subject: Good Old Days 263

Subject: Class of 2002

Just in case you weren't feeling old enough today, this will certainly change things. Each year the staff at Beloit College in Wisconsin puts together a list to try to give the Faculty a sense of the mindset of this year's incoming freshman.

Here is this year's list:

The people who are starting college this fall across the nation were born in 1983.

They have no meaningful recollection of the Reagan Era and probably did not know he had ever been shot.

They were prepubescent when the Persian Gulf War was waged.

There has been only one Pope in their lifetime.

They were 10 when the Soviet Union broke apart and do not remember the Cold War.

They are too young to remember the space shuttle blowing up.

Tianamen Square means nothing to them.

Bottle caps have always been screw off and plastic.

Atari predates them, as do vinyl albums.

The expression "You sound like a broken record" means nothing to them.

They have never owned a record player.

They have likely never played Pac Man and have never heard of Pong.

They may have never heard of an 8 track. The Compact Disc was introduced when they were 1 year old.

They have always had an answering machine.

Most have never seen a TV set with only 13 channels, nor have they seen a black and white TV.

They have always had cable.

There have always been VCRs, but they have no idea what BETA was.

They cannot fathom not having a remote control.

They don't know what a cloth baby diaper is, or know about the "Help me, I've fallen and I can't get up" commercial.

Feeling old Yet? There's more:

They were born the year that Walkmen were introduced by Sony.

Roller skating has always meant inline for them.

Jay Leno has always been on the Tonight Show.

They have no idea when or why Jordache jeans were cool.

Popcorn has always been cooked in the microwave.

They have never seen Larry Bird play.

261

Read This; It's Funny!!

They never took a swim and thought about Jaws.
The Vietnam War is as ancient history to them as WWI, WWII and the Civil War.
They have no idea that Americans were ever held hostage in Iran.
They can't imagine what hard contact lenses are.
They don't know who Mork was or where he was from. (The correct answer, by the way, is Ork)
They never heard: "Where's the beef?", "I'd walk a mile for a Camel," or "De plane, de plane!"
They do not care who shot J.R. and have no idea who J.R. was.
Michael Jackson has always been white.
Kansas, Chicago, Boston, America, and Alabama are places, not bands...
There has always been MTV.
They don't have a clue how to use a typewriter.
Do you feel old yet? If you do, then pass this on to some other old fogies... but don't send it back to me, I feel old enough.

Subject: Good Old Days

The following is an actual excerpt from a 1950 high school home-economics textbook:

Have dinner ready: Plan ahead, even the night before, to have a delicious meal on time. This is a way of letting him know that you have been thinking about and are concerned about his needs. Most men are hungry when they come home and the prospect of a good meal is part of the warm welcome needed.

Prepare yourself: Take fifteen minutes to rest so that you will be refreshed when he arrives. Touch up your make-up, put a ribbon in your hair and be fresh looking. He has just been with a lot of work-weary people. Be a little gay and a little more interesting. His boring day may need a lift.

Clean away the clutter: Make one last trip through the main part of the house just before your husband arrives, gathering up school books, toys, paper, etc. Then run a dust cloth over the tables. Your husband will feel he has reached a haven of rest and order, and it will give you a lift too.

Prepare the children: Take a few minutes to wash the children's hands and faces (if they are small), comb their hair, and if necessary change their clothes. They are little treasures and he would like to see them playing the part.

Minimize all noise: At the time of his arrival, eliminate all noise of the washer, dryer, dishwasher or vacuum. Try to encourage the children to be quiet. Be happy to see him. Greet him with a warm smile and be glad to see him.

Some don'ts: Don't greet him with problems or complaints. Don't complain if he is late for dinner. Count this as minor compared to what he might have gone through that day.

Make him comfortable. Have him lean back in a comfortable chair or suggest that he lie down in the bedroom. Have a cool or warm drink ready for him. Arrange his pillow and offer to take his shoes.

Speak in a low, soft, soothing voice. Allow him to relax and unwind. Listen to him: You may have a dozen things to tell him, but the moment of his arrival is not the time. Let him talk first.

Make the evening his: Never complain if he does not take you out to dinner or to other pleasant entertainment. Instead, try to understand his world of strain and pressure, his need to unwind and relax.

Read This; It's Funny!!

The goal: Try to make your home a place of peace and order where your husband can relax in body and spirit.

All of Your Business

Subject: New Element 266
Subject: Annual Christmas Party 267
Subject: Business Sense 270
Subject: Differences Between You and Your Boss 271
Subject: Heavenly Welcome 272
Subject: Reasons For Not Coming to Work 273
Subject: Restroom Rules 275
Subject: Multi-Cultural Bloopers 276

Read This; It's Funny!!

Subject: New Element

The University of California at Berkeley has recently announced the discovery of the heaviest element yet known to science. This new element has been tentatively named "Administratium". Administratium has 1 neutron, 12 assistant neutrons, 75 deputy neutrons, and 111 assistant deputy neutrons, giving it an atomic mass of 312. These 312 particles are held together by a force called morons, which are surrounded by vast quantities of lepton-like particles called peons.

Since Administratium has no electrons, it is inert. However, it can be detected as it impedes every reaction with which it comes into contact.

A minute amount of Administratium causes one reaction to take over 4 days to complete when it would normally take less than a second. Administratium has a normal half-life of 3 years; it does not decay but instead undergoes a reorganization, in which a portion of the assistant neutrons and deputy neutrons and assistant deputy neutrons exchange places.

In fact, Administratium's mass will actually increase over time, since each reorganization causes some morons to become neutrons forming isodopes.

This characteristic of moron-promotion leads some scientists to speculate that Administratium is formed whenever morons reach a certain quantity in concentration. This hypothetical quantity is referred to as "Critical Morass."

You will know it when you see it.

Subject: Annual Christmas Party

FROM: Pat Lewis, Human Resources Director
TO:Everyone
RE: Christmas Party
DATE: December 1

I'm happy to inform you that the company Christmas Party will take place on December 23, starting at noon in the banquet room at Luigi's Open Pit Barbecue. No-host bar, but plenty of eggnog!

We'll have a small band playing traditional carols...feel free to sing along.

And don't be surprised if our CEO shows up dressed as Santa Claus!

FROM: Pat Lewis, Human Resources Director
DATE: December 2
RE: Christmas Party

In no way was yesterday's memo intended to exclude our Jewish employees. We recognize that Chanukah is an important holiday which often coincides with Christmas, though unfortunately not this year. However, from now on we're calling it our "Holiday Party."

The same policy applies to employees who are celebrating Kwanzaa at this time. Happy now?

FROM: Pat Lewis, Human Resources Director
DATE: December 3
RE: Holiday Party

Regarding the note I received from a member of Alcoholics Anonymous requesting a non-drinking table ... you didn't sign your name. I'm happy to accommodate this request, but if I put a sign on a table that reads, "AA Only"; you wouldn't be anonymous anymore.

How am I supposed to handle this?

Somebody?

Read This; It's Funny!!

FROM: Pat Lewis, Human Resources Director
DATE: December 7
RE: Holiday Party

What a diverse company we are! I had no idea that December 20 begins the Muslim holy month of Ramadan, which forbids eating, drinking and sex during daylight hours. There goes the party!

Seriously, we can appreciate how a luncheon this time of year does not accommodate our Muslim employees' beliefs. Perhaps Luigi's can hold off on serving your meal until the end of the party - the days are so short this time of year - or else package everything for take-home in little foil swans.

Will that work? Meanwhile, I've arranged for members of Overeaters Anonymous to sit farthest from the dessert buffet and pregnant women will get the table closest to the restrooms. Did I miss anything?

FROM: Pat Lewis, Human Resources Director
DATE: December 8
RE: Holiday Party

So December 22 marks the Winter Solstice...what do you expect me to do, a tap-dance on your heads? Fire regulations at Luigi's prohibit the burning of sage by our "earth-based Goddess-worshipping" employees, but we'll try to accommodate your shamanic drumming circle during the band's breaks.

Okay???

FROM: Pat Lewis, Human Resources Director
Date: December 9
RE: Holiday Party

People, people, nothing sinister was intended by having our CEO dress up like Santa Claus! Even if the anagram of "Santa" does happen to be "Satan," there is no evil connotation to our own "little man in a red suit."

It's a tradition, folks, like sugar shock at Halloween or family feuds over the Thanksgiving turkey or broken hearts on Valentine's Day.

Could we lighten up?

FROM: Pat Lewis, Human Resources Director
DATE: December 10
RE: Holiday Party

Vegetarians!?!?!? I've had it with you people!!! We're going to keep this party at Luigi's Open Pit Barbecue whether you like it or not, so you can sit quietly at the table furthest from the "grill of death," as you so quaintly put it, and you'll get your #$%^&*! salad bar, including hydroponic tomatoes! But you know, they have feelings, too. Tomatoes scream when you slice them. I've heard them scream, I'm hearing them scream right now!

FROM: Teri Bishops, Acting Human Resources Director
DATE: December 14
RE: Pat Lewis and Holiday Party

I'm sure I speak for all of us in wishing Pat Lewis a speedy recovery from her stress-related illness and I'll continue to forward your cards to her at the sanatorium. In the meantime, management has decided to cancel our Holiday Party and give everyone the afternoon of the 23rd off with full pay.

Read This; It's Funny!!

Subject: Business Sense

A businessman was in a great deal of trouble. His business was failing, he had put everything he had into the business, he owed everybody - it was so bad he was even contemplating suicide.

As a last resort he went to a priest and poured out his story of tears and woe. When he had finished, the priest said, "Here's what I want you to do: Put a beach chair and your Bible in your car and drive down to the beach. Take the beach chair and the Bible to the water's edge, sit down in the beach chair, and put the Bible in your lap. Open the Bible; the wind will riffle the pages, but finally the open Bible will come to rest on a page. Look down at the page and read the first thing you see. That will be your answer, that will tell you what to do."

A year later the businessman went back to the priest and brought his wife and children with him. The man was in a new custom-tailored suit, his wife in a mink coat, the children shining. The businessman pulled an envelope stuffed with money out of his pocket, gave it to the priest as a donation in thanks for his advice.

The priest recognized the benefactor, and was curious.

"You did as I suggested?" he asked.

"Absolutely," replied the businessman.

"You went to the beach?"

"Absolutely."

"You sat in a beach chair with the Bible in your lap?"

"Absolutely."

"You let the pages riffle until they stopped?"

"Absolutely."

"And what were the first words you saw?"

"Chapter 11."

Subject: Differences Between You and Your Boss

When you take a long time, you're slow.
When your boss takes a long time, he's thorough.

When you don't do it, you're lazy.
When your boss doesn't do it, he's too busy.

When you make a mistake, you're an idiot.
When your boss makes a mistake, he's only human.

When doing something without being told, you're overstepping
your authority.
When your boss does the same thing, that's initiative.

When you take a stand, you're being bull-headed.
When your boss does it, he's being firm.

When you overlooked a rule of etiquette, you're being rude.
When your boss skips a few rules, he's being original.

When you please your boss, you're apple polishing.
When your boss pleases his boss, he's being co-operative.

When you're out of the office, you're wandering around.
When your boss is out of the office, he's on business.

When you're on a day off sick, you're always sick.
When your boss is a day off sick, he must be very ill.

When you apply for leave, you must be going for an interview.
When your boss applies for leave, it's because he's overworked.

Read This; It's Funny!!

Subject: Heavenly Welcome

A contractor dies in a car accident on his 40th birthday and finds himself at the Pearly Gates. A brass band is playing, the Angels are singing a beautiful hymn, there is a huge crowd cheering and shouting his name and absolutely everyone wants to shake his hand. Just when he thinks things can't possibly get any better, Saint Peter himself runs over, apologizes for not greeting him personally at the Pearly Gates, shakes his hand and says, "Congratulations son, we've been waiting a long time for you!"

Totally confused and a little embarrassed, the contractor sheepishly looks at Saint Peter and says, 'Saint Peter, I tried to lead a God fearing life, I loved my family, I tried to obey the 10 Commandments, but congratulations for what? I honestly don't remember doing anything really special when I was alive."

"Congratulations for what?" says Saint Peter, totally amazed at the man's modesty. "We're celebrating the fact that you lived to be 160 years old! God, himself, wants to see you!"

The contractor is awestruck and can only look at Saint Peter with his mouth agape. When he regains his power of speech, he looks up at Saint Peter and says, "'Saint Peter, I lived my life in the eternal hope that when I died I would be judged by God and be found to be worthy, but I only lived to be forty."

"That's simply impossible, son," says Saint Peter. "We've added up all the hours on your time sheets."

Subject: Reasons For Not Coming to Work

CREDIT: The Washington Post contest: "Best Reasons for not coming to work"

-When I got up this morning I took two Ex-Lax in addition to my Prozac. I can't get off the john, but I feel good about it.

- I set half the clocks in my house ahead an hour and the other half back an hour Saturday and spent 18 hours in some kind of space-time continuum loop, reliving Sunday (right up until the explosion). I was able to exit the loop only by reversing the polarity of the power source exactly e*log(pi) clocks in the house while simultaneously rapping my dog on the snout with a rolled up Times. Accordingly, I will be in late, or early.

- My stigma's acting up.

- I have a rare case of 48-hour projectile leprosy, but I know we have that deadline to meet...

- I am stuck in the blood pressure machine down at the Wal-Mart.

- Yes, I seem to have contracted some attention-deficit disorder and, hey, how about them Skins, huh? So, I won't be able to, yes, could I help you? No, no, I'll be sticking with AT&T, but thank you for calling.

- Constipation has made me a walking time bomb.

- I just found out that I was switched at birth. Legally, I shouldn't come in to work knowing my employee records may now contain false information.

- The psychiatrist said it was an excellent session. He even gave me this jaw restraint so I won't bite things when I am startled.

- The dog ate my car keys. We're going to hitchhike to the vet.

- I prefer to remain an enigma.

Read This; It's Funny!!

- My mother-in-law has come back as one of the undead and we must track her to her coffin to drive a stake through her heart and give her eternal peace. One day should do it.

- I can't come to work today because the EPA has determined that my house is completely surrounded by wetlands and I have to arrange for helicopter transportation.

- I am converting my calendar from Julian to Gregorian.

- I am extremely sensitive to a rise in the interest rates.

- My wife makes more money than I do, so I have to stay at home with our sick son.

- I refuse to travel to my job in the district until there is a commuter tax. I insist on paying my fair share.

- I'm feeling a little disgruntled this morning. You sure I should come in?

- If it is all the same to you I won't be coming to work. The voices told me to clean all the guns today.

- I can't come in to work today because I'll be stalking my previous boss who fired me for not showing up for work. Ok?

274

Subject: Restroom Rules

TO: ALL EMPLOYEES

SUBJECT: NEW RESTROOM PROCEDURES

In the past, employees were permitted to make trips to the restroom under informal guidelines. Effective the beginning of next month, a Restroom Trip Policy (RTP) will be established to provide a consistent method of accounting for each employee's restroom times and ensuring equal treatment of all employees.

Under this policy, a "RESTROOM TRIP BANK" will be established for each employee. The first day of the month. Employees will be given a Restroom Trip Credit of 20. Restroom credits can be accumulated from month to month.

Starting next month, the entrance of all restrooms will be equipped with personnel identification stations and computer-linked voice print recognition devices. Before the end of the month, each employee must provide two copies of voice prints (one normal, one under stress) to the System Operator. The voice print recognition stations will be operational but not restrictive, for the first month; employees should acquaint themselves with the stations during that period.

In an employee's RESTROOM TRIP BANK balance reaches zero, the doors of the restroom will not unlock for the employee's voice until the first of the next month. In addition, all restroom stalls are being equipped with timed paper roll retractors. If the stall is occupied for more than three minutes, an alarm will sound. Thirty seconds after the alarm sounds, the roll of paper in the stall will retract, the toilet will flush and the stall door will open. If the stall remains occupied, your picture will be taken.

The picture will then be posted on the bulletin board located outside the lunch room. This is being done to eliminate "dilly-dallying" in the restrooms. Anyone whose picture shows up three times will immediately be terminated.

If you have any questions about the new policy, please ask your supervisor.

Read This; It's Funny!!

Subject: Multi-Cultural Bloopers

The nominees for the Chevy Nova Award, named in Honor of the GM's fiasco in trying to market this car in Central and South America. "no va" means, of course, in Spanish, "it doesn't go"

---

1. The Dairy Association's huge success with the campaign "Got milk?" prompted them to expand advertising to Mexico. It was soon brought to their attention the Spanish translation read "Are you lactating?"

2. Coors put its slogan, "Turn It Loose," into Spanish, where it was read as "Suffer From Diarrhea".

3. Scandinavian vacuum manufacturer Electrolux used the following in an American campaign, "Nothing sucks like an Electrolux".

4. Clairol introduced the "Mist Stick," a curling iron, into Germany only to find out that "mist" is slang for manure.

5. When Gerber started selling baby food in Africa, they used the same packaging as in the US, with the smiling baby on the label. Later they learned that in Africa, companies routinely put pictures on the labels of what's inside, since many people can't read.

6. Colgate introduced a toothpaste in France called Cue, the name of a notorious porno magazine.

7. An American T-shirt maker in Miami printed shirts for the Spanish market which promoted the Pope's visit Instead of "I Saw the Pope" (el Papa), the shirts read "I Saw the Potato" (la papa).

8. Pepsi's "Come Alive With the Pepsi Generation" translated into "Pepsi Brings Your Ancestors Back From the Grave" in Chinese.

9. The Coca-Cola name in China was first read as "Kekoukela", meaning "Bite the wax tadpole" or "female horse stuffed with wax", depending on the dialect. Coke then researched 40,000 characters to find a phonetic equivalent "kokou kole", translating into "happiness in the mouth".

10. Frank Perdue's chicken slogan, "It takes a strong man to make a tender chicken" was translated into Spanish as "it takes an aroused man to make a chicken affectionate".

11. When Parker Pen marketed a ball-point pen in Mexico, its ads were supposed to have read, "It won't leak in your pocket and embarrass you". The company thought that the word "embarazar" (to impregnate) meant to embarrass, so the ad read: "It won't leak in your pocket and make you pregnant!"

12. When American Airlines wanted to advertise its new leather first class seats in the Mexican market, it translated its "Fly In Leather" campaign literally, which meant "Fly Naked" (vuela en cuero) in Spanish.

What We Have Learned

Subject: Rules of Life 279
Subject: Leadership 280
Subject: Take a Letter 281

Subject: Rules of Life

Sometimes we just need to remember WHAT the RULES of LIFE really are...

1. Never give yourself a haircut after three margaritas.

2. You need only two tools: WD-40 and duct tape. If it doesn't move and it should, use WD-40. If it moves and shouldn't, use the tape.

3. The five most essential words for a healthy, vital relationship are "I apologize" and "You are right."

4. Everyone seems normal until you get to know them.

5. When you make a mistake, make amends immediately. It's easier to eat crow while it's still warm.

6. The only really good advice that your mother ever gave you was: "Go! You might meet somebody!"

7. If he/she says that you are too good for him/her—believe them.

8. Learn to pick your battles; ask yourself, 'Will this matter one year from now? How about one month? One week? One day?'

9. Never pass up an opportunity to pee.

10. If you woke up breathing, congratulations! You have another chance!

11. Living well really is the best revenge. Being miserable because of a bad or former relationship just might mean that the other person was right about you.

12. Work is good, but it's not that important.

13. And finally... be really nice to your friends and family. You never know when you are going to need them to empty your bedpan.

Read This; It's Funny!!

Subject: Leadership

Long ago lived a seaman named Captain Bravo. He was a manly man's man who showed no fear in facing his enemies. One day, while sailing the seven seas, a lookout spotted a pirate ship and the crew became frantic.

Captain Bravo bellowed, "Bring me my red shirt."

The First Mate quickly retrieved the captain's red shirt and while wearing the bright garment he led his crew into battle and defeated the pirates.

Later on, the lookout again spotted not one, but two pirate ships.

The captain again howled for his red shirt and once again vanquished the pirates.

That evening, all the men sat around on the deck recounting the day's triumphs and one of the them asked the captain: "Sir, why do you call for your red shirt before battle?"

The captain replied: "If I am wounded in the attack, the shirt will not show my blood, and thus, you men will continue to resist, unafraid."

All of the men sat in silence and marveled at the courage of such a manly man's man.

As dawn came the next morning, the lookout once again spotted not one, not two, but TEN pirate ships approaching. The rank and file all stared in worshipful silence at the captain and waited for his usual reply.

Captain Bravo gazed with steely eyes upon the vast armada arrayed against his mighty sailing ship and, without fear, turned and calmly shouted: "Get me my brown pants."

Subject: Take a Letter

This is creepy

Think of a letter between A and W.

Repeat it out loud as you scroll down.

Keep going . . . Don't stop . . .

Think of an animal that begins with that letter.

Repeat it out loud as you scroll down.

Think of a man's/woman's name that begins with the last letter in the animals name

Almost there........

Now count out the letters in that name on the fingers of the hand you are not using to scroll down.

Take the hand you counted with and hold it out in front of you at face level

Look at you palm very closely and notice the lines in your hand

Do the lines take the form of the first letter in the person's name?

Of course not.......

Now smack yourself in the head, get a life, and quit playing stupid e-mail games!

Index

A

A Christmas Poem 27
Actual Headlines 71
Airlines 173
Anagrams 111
Annual Christmas Party 267

B

Bad Day 219
Baseball In Heaven? 207
Because I'm A Guy 154
Before Children/After Children 43
Behind Every Great Inventor 145
Benefits of Being a Senior 194
Birthdays and Time 177
Blond Revenge 95
Brain Exercise 77
Brilliant 254
Broker's Tips 112
Bumper Stickers 1 64
Bumper Stickers 2 67
Business Sense 270
Buy It! 146

C

Car Jacker 197
Cat Wisdom 113
Chocolate is a Vegetable 114
Christmas Intent 56
Cigars 230
Class of 2002 261
Computer Gender 83
Computer Haiku 84
Cost of Kids 45
Cute Signs 68

D

Daffynitions 115
Deteriorata 58
Differences Between a Man and a Woman 156
Differences Between You and Your Boss 271
Discoveries of the Sexes 157
Do You Have A.A.A.D.D? 130
Dr. Seuss Tech 86

E

Email From Heaven 218
Even More Puns 5
Exercise is Good For You 176

F

Fore!!! 148
Found Money 193

G

Gender 120
Getting Old 196
Girls Raised in the South 243
Golf 208
Good Old Days 263
Great Truths For Adults 257

H

Heart to Heart 149
Heavenly Welcome 272
Hero 97
How to Annoy People 104
How to Handle Stress 102
How To Keep A Healthy Level Of Insanity 108
How to Screw Up an Interview 106
How-to Classes For Men 158

I

I Think Santa Claus is a Woman.... 35
I'm a Senior Citizen 201

Instructions for Life 60
It's a Texas Thing 252

J

Jail 96
Jedi Mind Trick 79
Just a Mother 47

K

Kid Wisdom 18
Kids on Relationships 15

L

LAZY Virus 87
Leadership 280
Leonard and the Devil 200
Lesson for the Day 49
Letter to a Bank 136
Letter to the IRS 139
Life Quips 178
Little Hints and Sayings 179

M

Marriage Quotes 152
Merry Christmas, Legally Speaking 26
Michael the Dragon Master 217
Moods of a Woman 160
More Daffynitions 116
More Wisdom 181
Movin to Texas? 232
Moving to Arizona 220
Mr. & Mrs. Potato 2
Multi-Cultural Bloopers 276
Mustard 50
Mutterings 175
My Class Reunion 214

N

New Dog Cross Breeds 118
New Element 266

O

On the Next Edition of "Survivor" 164
Open Letter to Women 161

P

Perfection 168
Pillsbury Doughboy 100
Please Egcuse My Child 13
Please Help 222
Politically Correct Ways to Call Someone Stupid 182
Ponder This 2 184
Potty Humor 51
Priorities 209
Puns 3

Q

Questions for the Wise 122
Quick Eye Exam 81

R

Raging River 163
Rat Race Explained 227
Really Awfully Bad Writing 22
Reasons For Not Coming to Work 273
Redneck Etiquette 235
Redneck Valentines Day Poem 237
Rejected Hallmark Cards 75
Remember When 88
Restroom Rules 275
Right Age for Cussing 101
Rod and Reel 98
Rules for Writers 123
Rules of Life 279

S

Santa and the Angel 37
Santa's New Contract 38
Sarcastic Remarks to Get You Through the Day 186
Science Exam Quotes 19
Senior Driver 198
Sharing Everything 205
Snow 224
Some Things For You to Ponder 183
Somebody Said 52
Southern Advice 240
Southern Expressions 242
Southern Knowledge 246
Special Pig 99
Spell Checker 89
Sports Geniuses 210
Stewart to Bombeck 142
Still More Puns 7
Still More Quips 188

T

10 Ways To Terrify A Telemarketer 109
12 Days of Christmas 30
T-Shirt Slogans 72
Take a Letter 281
Tech Support 171
Texas First Aid 248
Thanksgiving Weather 40
The Hills 9
The Month After Christmas 29
The Night Before Thanksgiving 24
The Y1K Crisis 128
There Was This Guy 8
Things Your Mother Wouldn't Say 54
Those People from Maine 199
To Be Six, Again 151
Today's Stock Market Report 125
Top Ten 165
Try This 62

U

Useful Conflict Resolution Phrases 189

W

Weather by Degree 126
What Does She Do? 11
What Moms REALLY Want 41
What's in the Box 150
Where's Ethyl? 228
Who's on Start? 90
Why it's Great to be a Man 166
Why Parents Have Gray Hair 55
Windows Southern Edition.. 92
Wisdom From Senior Citizens 203
Wisdom of Will Rogers 190
Women's T-Shirts.. 70
Words of Wisdom 191
Working Puns 4

Y

You Know You're a Texan When 249
You Know You're Not a Kid Anymore If 131
You Might be a Redneck Jedi if 251
You Worked During the 90's If 132
Young King Arthur 169
You've Been Out of College Too Long When 134

Z

Zen 258